WHY IS MONEY BAD FOR YOU?

ROBERT WYETH

WORKBOOK PRESS LLC
187 E Warm Springs Rd,
Suite B285, Las Vegas, NV 89119, USA

Website: https://workbookpress.com/
Hotline: 1-888-818-4856
Email: admin@workbookpress.com

Ordering Information:
Quantity sales. Special discounts are available on quantity purchases by corporations, associations, and others.
For details, contact the publisher at the address above.

ISBN-13:   978-1-953839-19-0 (Paperback Version)
              978-1-953839-18-3 (Digital Version)

REV. DATE: 08/31/2022

Why Is Money Bad For You?

Robert Wyeth

Contents

Acknowledgements

Most of the verses were taken from the NIV Bible:

The Holy Bible, New International Version®, copyright 1973, 1978, 1984 by International Bible Society.

Copyright 1985 by the Zondervan Corporation.

Anglicisation 1987 by the Hodder and Stoughton Limited.

This edition first presented in Great Britain in 1987.

Other versions:

Holy Bible, New Living Translation ®, copyright © 1996, 2004 by Tyndale Charitable Trust, issued by the Tyndale House Publishers.

The Holy Bible containing the Old and New Testaments the New King James Version. Copyright © 1979, 1980 by Thomas Nelson Inc. Published by Broadman & Holman Publishers, Nashville. Tennessee.

It contains the 1611 version of the Authorised Version for the Holy Scriptures.

No one can serve two masters.

Either he will hate the one and love the other,

or he will be devoted to the one and despise the other.

You cannot serve both God and Money.

Matthew ch.6 v24

All the believers were together

and had everyone in common,

Selling their possessions and goods,

they gave to anyone as he had need ...

the Lord added to their number daily

those who were being saved.

Acts ch.2 v44-45, v47

Summary

Sometimes wealth might come to the believer, but it is hard to work for the Lord with great riches. What can we do with it? Share it out? Who gets what? What about the starving people on earth? Put it in the bank? Invest it? Our treasures are not on this earth but in heaven. Riches and property are what the unbeliever prides himself with getting more and more prosperity. You work hard and get more money. You cheat and assets will come eventually. Violence will always be there, whether you like it or not. If you have more property, then the poor will have less.

God watches everyone closely, examining every person on earth. The Lord examines both the righteous and the wicked. Psalm ch.14 v4-5 (NLT)

The Lord watches everyone closely that means he sees everything, what you get up to in your house or down the pub. Nothing will escape from him and God writes it down. The way of the Lord is not like that. The wicked person on earth his 'soul hates', he considers that this is not the person he wants to be in his kingdom of heaven. Jesus let the rich young man, who asked him, "How do I get to heaven?"

He (The rich young man) went away sad, because he had great wealth. Mark ch.10 v22

Jesus told him, "To sell everything you have and give it to the poor." He didn't go after him, he let him go. He didn't send his disciples after him, he looked and watched him go. The young man wanted to come and go to heaven but he was deeply saddened. You don't hear what happened to the rich young man, he did not come to Jesus. He remained on this earth deeply worried, because he had wealth and didn't share it with the poor.

I am not saying that a believer has to give it all away. It was very hard with money, wealth and estates. A believer has the Holy Spirit but he will guide you what to do with it.

Abundance

Abundance is as an ample sufficiency or a great plenty.

In the Old Testament, God has given the Israelites a lot of good things. They were chosen by God for his possession on earth. Like soil to plant from, the goods from grapes and olives, more flocks of sheep and oxen. However, they fully obeyed the word of the Lord (see Deuteronomy ch.28 v1-14). They depended on obeying God first, if they didn't do that, disaster will come upon them and they will be taken away as captives.

Isaac said to Esau, "I have made Jacob your master and have declared that all his brothers will be his servants. I have guaranteed him an abundance of grain and wine—what is left for me to give you, my son?" Genesis ch.27 v37 (NLT)

Isaac had two boys. Esau became a skilful hunter while Jacob stayed at home (see Genesis ch.25 v27). They each went to their father to receive a blessing, because their father gave his sons his approval or dedication. Esau gave his birthright away for some lentil soup because he was hungry, he spurned it as his right to get Isaac's blessing (see Genesis ch.25 v29-34).

Jacob went in first because Isaac could not see, for he was old. Isaac blessed Jacob thinking he was Esau because he was away hunting game for Isaac. Esau was not happy with Jacob he tried to murder him.

- - - - - - - -

You crown the year with a bountiful harvest; even the hard pathways overflow with abundance. The grasslands of the wilderness become a lush pasture, and the hillsides blossom with joy. The meadows are clothed with flocks of sheep, and the valleys are carpeted with grain. Psalm ch.65 v11-13 (NLT)

King David had a song that he wrote down. David and his brothers were shepherds looking after the sheep for his father (see 1 Samuel ch.16 v11-12). But he was the youngest of his brothers but became a king over Israel. He was the kind of man who was gentle and fierce, he ruled the land and expanded his country. But he was close to God and wrote many things in the book of Psalms. He knew and understood what God had done.

- - - - - - - -

You subdued them before the Canaanites, who lived in the land ... They captured fortified cities and fertile land; they took possession of house filled with all kinds of good things, wells already dug, vineyards, olive groves and fruit trees in abundance. They ate to the full and were well-nourished they revelled in your great goodness. Nehemiah ch.9 v24-25

Nehemiah was thinking about the Israelites. They had gone away under the exile for over 1200 years since Isaac blessed Jacob. The people in the land had not obeyed the Lord God; several kings they were corrupted and failed to do what God wanted. Back now in the Promised Land, they built the temple and walls around Jerusalem which were in ruins since the Babylonian empire had sacked and burnt them down.

Nehemiah was thinking about the past, his forefathers where they went into the Promised Land. It was all so good. But now they started again with the land stretched out before them. Nothing there in the land, the fields were overgrown and the shrubs and trees were neglected.

- - - - - - - -

In the New Testament it will be different again, the abundance is through knowledge.

Jesus replied, "The knowledge of the secrets of the kingdom of heaven has been given to you, but not to them. Whoever has will be given more, and he will have an abundance. Whoever does not have, even what he has will be taken from him." Matthew ch.13 v11-12

Jesus disciples asked him, 'Why did he speak to the people in parables'. Like the parable of the Sower who went out sowing seed. Some fell on the path, some fell of rock soil, some fell on thorns and some fell on the good soil. Jesus answered, 'The knowledge of the kingdom of God has been given to you, but not to the crowd'.

Jesus used parables as a means of teaching. They were effective and easily remembered because he used familiar scenes. They also included hidden meanings that needing further exploration. He taught truths that Jesus wanted to conceal from unbelievers. It was through knowledge that the disciples understood.

- - - - - - - -

Jesus said, "Take the talent from him and give it to the one who has the ten talents. For everyone who has will be given more, and he will have an abundance." Matthew ch.25 v28-29

The parable of the Talents. Some work hard on this earth and gave up ten talents to the master. Others work positively and will give up five talents. But the one who didn't give any talents at all he made an excuse why he didn't bother. So the Father said, 'Give the talents to the one who worked hard, it is a reward for his work.'

It is not the kind of work that we do here on earth, it is a reward for the heavenly gifts that only come when we do the will of the Holy Spirit. We might not go out and do missionary work or speaking to the crowd or helping in the church because we are not well; we are in a wheelchair, or blind or have cancer. But the Holy Spirit looks at each one and gives him or her a task to do that equals ten talents. Do you understand that I am trying to say? It is the fruit that the Holy Spirit gives each one personally.

- - - - - - - -

From his abundance we have all received one gracious blessing after another. For the law was given through Moses, but God's unfailing love and faithfulness came through Jesus Christ. John ch.1 v16-17 (NLT)

The love of God who manifested himself in Jesus Christ. The Lord loves us faithfully, when we come to Jesus to receive him as Lord and Saviour. But

God's law stands today and we must follow Jesus. This is an abundance of knowledge that we possess, when we do the right things for his heavenly kingdom. That only we must do.

Belongings

Belongings is a person of values and lifestyle. Conforming to social, accepted standards of behaviour.

So Jacob put his wives and children on camels, and he drove all his livestock in front of him. He packed all the belongings he had acquired in Paddan-aram and set out for the land of Canaan, where his father Isaac, lived. Genesis ch.31 v17-18 (NLT)

Jacob, he went away to his family in Haran (see Genesis ch.28 v10), about 300 miles away from the Promised Land and married two girls, Leah and Rebekah. He worked for Laban for fourteen years work herding the sheep to get the rights of marriage to his girls. Jacob tricked Laban and he was furious with him. His sons were saying, 'Jacob has taken what belonged to us'. So Jacob departed and returned home without saying goodbye. He packed all his belongings on the camels, took his wives and children and herded the sheep before him.

It was later, when Joseph was master over Egypt.

They also took all their livestock and all the personal belongings they had acquired in the land of Canaan. So Jacob and his entire family went to Egypt— sons and grandsons, daughters and granddaughters—all his descendants. Genesis ch.46 v6-7 (NLT)

When Jacob discovered Joseph was indeed master over all Egypt. He thought he might be dead, because that's what his sons were saying (see Genesis ch.37 v32-33). Joseph was precious to him and he gave him an ornamental robe, a mark of Jacob's favouritism. So Jacob went to Egypt and his entire family all of his personal belongings. Joseph had sent carts for him for his belongings to see him (see Genesis ch.45 v27).

- - - - - - - -

Israel has sinned and broken my covenant! They have stolen some of the things that I commanded must be set apart for me. And they have not only stolen them but have lied about it and hidden the things among their own belongings. Joshua ch.7 v11 (NLT).

When the Israelites moved into the Promised Land, they surrounded Jericho because no-one went out and no-one went in, the gates were tightly shut (see Joshua ch.6 v1). The Israelites went round the city for six days with the ark of the covenant but the people remained silent. On the seventh day the people shouted and the trumpet sounded and the walls collapsed. The Israelites were told not to take the gold, silver, bronze and iron they must go into the treasury of the Lord. It was the Lord who had collapsed the walls.

But Achan of the tribe of Judah sinned. He removed the gold and silver and hid them in his own possessions. He didn't tell anyone.

- - - - - - - -

When Nehemiah was governor over the remnant that had returned to the Promised Land.

I became very upset and threw all of Tobiah's belongings out of the room. Then I demanded that the rooms be purified, and I brought back the articles for God's Temple, the grain offerings, and the frankincense. Nehemiah ch.13 v8-9 (NLT)

When the exile for the Israelites was over, they went back to build the temple of the Lord God. However, Tobiah the Ammonite official was very disturbed that someone had come to promote the welfare of the Israelites (see Nehemiah ch.2 v10). He was angry and caused trouble for the Israelites.

Meanwhile, Eliashib the priest had been put in charge of the storerooms of the temple and he had been closely associated with Tobiah. He had provided him with a large room formerly used to store the grain offerings and incense and temple articles and as well as contribution for the Levites and priests (see Nehemiah ch.13 v4-5).

Tobiah was not really religious but political, he was upset by Nehemiah's influence. So, Nehemiah threw him out of the temple and his belongings.

- - - - - - - -

For when a strong man like Satan is fully armed and guards his palace, his possessions are safe—until someone even stronger attacks and overpowers him, strips him of his weapons, and carries off his belongings. Luke ch.11 v21-22 (NLT)

Jesus was explaining to the crowds, when Satan has all his possessions safely guarded, he is fully armed and his palace to protect the goods. It is not Satan who is immeasurably strong, but if one overcomes him, he will take all his possessions away and leave Satan powerless. This is how he can be overcome, cast into an abyss or even hell itself. He will be without power and unable to fight against one stronger than him.

The possessions of Satan included all his wealth and power. Do we know where it is? It is all of the assets of his servants, the kings, rulers and the masses of people who were sinning (see Luke ch.20 v23-25).

- - - - - - - -

A few days later this younger son packed all his belongings and moved to a distant land, and there he wasted all his money in wild living. Luke ch.15 v13 (NLT)

The parable of the Lost Son. The younger one went to his father to give him the share of the estate. He should not have had it, only when the father is dead the firstborn son inherits all of from share of the estate. Anyway, he divided his property among the two of them. Not long after that, the younger son got together with all that he had. He set off for a distant country and squandered all of it in 'wild living'. The property was still in the father's name, but he divided it up so the younger son had an awful lot of money. The son's motive becomes apparent when he departs, taking with him all his possessions and leaving nothing behind to come back to. He wants to be free from parental restraint, to spend his share of the family wealth as he pleases.

The elder son said to his father, 'You never gave me a goat for my friends and I've been slaving for you each day. But this son of yours who has been living with prostitutes comes home, you kill the fatted calf for him'. But the father says, 'We had to celebrate because this younger son was dead but he is alive again'. The possessions allow him to be dead towards his family, it was a distant country, far away.

This was a great shame because the possessions mean that we will be dead towards God and not even realise it. Our possessions mean that we are solely interested in them and darkness is all around us, so that we can't see the truth and what it means for us (see Matthew ch.6 v10-24).

Crowns

Crowns is a circular head ornament especially as a mark of honour. The diadem of royalty and the governing power in a monarchy.

For the Lord takes delight in his people; he crowns the humble with salvation. Psalm ch.149 v4

For the Lord takes delight in his people. His people who he rescued them for slavery out of Egypt, he delivered them from slavery out of Babylon, only a remnant of Judah was there. The great majority of Jews of the final generation will be saved, provided they accept Jesus as their Lord and Saviour. He gives them each a crown as a mark of honour.

- - - - - - - -

For what is our hope, our joy, or the crown in which we will glory in the presence of our Lord Jesus Christ when he comes? Is that not you? Indeed, you are our glory and joy. 1 Thessalonians ch.2 v19

The apostle Paul always thanks God for the Thessalonica church which had a large number of God-fearing Greeks and not a few prominent women (see Acts ch.17 v4). He explained that our crowns which we will have in the coming of the Lord Jesus. Everyone had a crown, even the Greeks.

Our hope and our joy is this, that we await our precious Lord which will be glorious. Timothy who is Paul's fellow-worker in the faith.

- - - - - - - -

Now there is in store for me the crown of righteousness, which the Lord, the righteous Judge, will award to me on that day - and not only to me, but also to all who have longed for his appearing. 2 Timothy ch.4 v8

The apostle Paul was in prison awaiting to see the Emperor Nero to explain what he had not done in the temple in Jerusalem. Nero was a bully and subject to cruelty. He ordered that the city of Rome be set on fire and then charged the Christians with carrying it out.

Paul didn't know what the outcome was, but he was confident that for him the crown of righteousness which the Lord will award to him on that day. When Jesus returns to oust Satan and save his people. Regretfully, Paul lost his life, but had over two years to preach and teach the gospel of our Lord Jesus Christ (see Acts ch.28 v30-31).

- - - - - - - -

When the Chief Shepherd appears, you will receive the crown of glory that will never fade away. 1 Peter ch.5 v4

Jesus will come back and reward all of those with the crown of glory.

Glory: it will be to glorify God, like in worship. Adore and honour God for what he has done. We are sinners and should have not been going to heaven, but God in his magnificence chose us, we can be like Jesus heirs of the living God. It is a phrase most distinguished and renowned that we are heirs of God, we will take our place for eternity. It is splendid, beautiful and perfect bodies which don't age and are healthy, not diseased and the muscles work easily for what we will have to do.

This crown can never fade away. It will be still like that for ever and ever. Our new bodies will still be there, like the angels' bodies. You don't see the angels getting old or infirm in the Bible. They will still be there praising God and doing his work.

- - - - - - - -

Blessed in the man who perseveres under trial, because when he has stood the test, he will receive the crown of life that God has promised to those who love him. James ch.1 v12

The crown of life that God has promised for the one who has stood firm under trial. Whatever the trial may be: like illness, being alone, working hard, being in prison for Jesus, being beaten for the truth, having nothing at all and praising God.

What is the 'crown of life' like?

Life: it is an existence far beyond what we are doing on this earth. Jesus promised his disciples that they will judge on their thrones looking after

Israel (see Matthew ch.19 v28). Anyone who has left everything for Jesus' sake will receive a hundred times as much in eternal life (see Matthew ch.19 v29). We are not sure what it means, but life means experience, activities, travelling and meeting people. Not sitting alone in your hut or house but getting out (see Matthew ch.28 v19-20).

Be faithful, even to the point of death, and I will give you the crown of life. Revelation ch.2 v10

Be faithful even to the point of death. Even in the Bible, Jesus points to 'carry the cross for him'. Inevitably facing death because Satan the enemy is trying to win you to get you back on his path. Death in Jesus is what we hope for like in the book of Hebrews:

Others were tortured and refused to be released, so that they might gain a better resurrection. Hebrews ch.11 v35

Paul said, "Yet we live on; beaten, and yet not killed; sorrowful, yet always rejoicing; poor yet making many rich; having nothing, and yet possessing everything." 2 Corinthians ch.6 v9-10

I have worked much harder, been in prison more frequently, been flogged more severely, and been exposed to death again and again. Five times I received from the Jews the forty lashes minus one. Three times I was beaten with rods. 2 Corinthians ch.11 v23-25

The believers' life is hard on this earth and Satan and the fallen angels are trying to destroy you. When Jesus comes again, it will all be forgotten when he presents us with a crown and we can see that it is all worth doing.

Fortune

Fortune is a great accumulation of wealth or a large amount of money.

"I am Abraham's servant," he explained. "The Lord has greatly blessed my master; he has become a wealthy man. The Lord has given him flocks of sheep and goats, herds of cattle, a fortune in silver and gold, and many male and female servants and camels and donkeys." Genesis ch.24 v34-35 (NLT)

Abraham was 'now old and well advanced in years', the Lord had blessed him in many ways (see Genesis ch.24 v1). Abraham's chief servant was going to get a wife for Isaac his son. Not from the daughters of the Canaanites, but go back to the country of the people of Mesopotamia to my own relatives.

So the servant went off, it was a journey of about 500 miles. He went to the well in the town of Nahor, the time when the women went out to draw water (see Genesis ch.24 v10-11). He prayed to the Lord and before he had finished praying Rebekah came out of the town. He asked if there was room in her house for him to stay. Laban was her brother and he saw the gold things that Rebekah was wearing (see Genesis ch.24 v29). The servant told him what he was about to ask and they said it was from the Lord, take Rebekah and go (see Genesis ch.24 v50-51).

- - - - - - - -

Israel boasts, "I am rich! I've made a fortune all by myself! No one has caught me cheating! My record is spotless!" But I am the Lord your God, who rescued you from slavery in Egypt. "And I will make you live in tents again, as you do each year at the Festival of Shelters. I sent my prophets to warn you with many visions and parables." Hosea ch.12 v8-10 (NLT)

The prophet Hosea prophesied during which six kings were murdered by their successors while in office. It was the last days of Israel before the exile. Hosea's ministry began by warning people that the Assyrian Empire was going to destroy Israel, because they didn't understand they forgot that disloyalty with God was spiritual adultery.

Riches brought self-sufficiency. Like a dishonest merchant, Israel was confident that her deceitfulness would not be found out. God had sent his prophets and there had been ample warning from the Lord. This was going to be slavery yet again, like in Egypt.

Gains

Gains are to one's advantage, to be successful, to become better than all the others.

It is the picture of what one can see in one's life. You start with understanding as you come to Jesus and ask him what should you do? Then wealth comes as you get older and if you are more concerned with that, it consumes you. After that, when you die in the future, what will happen to you?

Blessed is the man who finds wisdom, the man who gains understanding, for she is more profitable than silver and yields better returns than gold. Proverbs ch.3 v13-14

The same claim for the commands and precept of the Lord. What is better than gold or silver? They each have a tarnish that does not fade or rust. Understanding is far better than even gold.

For the 'Time Team' on the television they unearthed a gold sovereign from the time of the Tudors. Somebody had dropped it while going over the wooden plank there was a moat around the castle. Suddenly after they cleaned it the gold was there and all of the team were astonished; all the details of the coin were there. Nobody had even found a real gold coin of that age. 'Blessed is the man who finds wisdom, the man who gains understanding' this is true for buried treasure, but you will only find it by looking and studying the Bible.

Understanding is also found in Proverbs ch.8 v10, v19 and ch.16 v16. It is important that you find what you are looking for. 'Understanding' is truly more than gold or silver could buy.

- - - - - - - -

A kind-hearted woman gains respect, but ruthless men gain only wealth. Proverbs ch.11 v16

A good name is more desirable than great riches. The woman perceives that if she is kind-hearted, will be accorded more respect than wealthy men if they are ruthless. A woman who fears the Lord is to be praised (see Proverbs ch.31 v28-31).

You don't have to be rich and get even more wealth. Ruthless men get rich quicker by taking advantage over the poor who didn't even have a place to go. The woman thought respect for her life but the ruthless man only thought of wealth.

- - - - - - - -

Unlike the past, invaders will not take their houses and confiscate their vineyards. For my people will live as long as trees, and my chosen ones will have time to enjoy their hard-won gains. They will not work in vain, and their children will not be doomed to misfortune. Isaiah ch.65 v22-23 (NLT)

When you die there will be a separation from the good and the bad all souls will go immediately back to God. This is why the dead can't talk or respond. The body is gone and their elements or dust will pass into the ground. God didn't make it like that, sin entered the world and therefore we all have to die (see Genesis ch.3 v19).

God will allow his precious children or heirs to work and live as long as trees.

"As the days of a tree, so will be the days of my people". Isaiah ch.65 v22

You don't think of the life of trees. I know a yew tree and it only shoots about a few inches per year. How big is the yew tree when it is grown? Then after the judgement by God, the trees will last for ever. Their gains will last for eternity.

- - - - - - - -

Jesus said, "He will separate the people one from another as a shepherd separates the sheep from the goats. He will put the sheep on his right hand and the goats on his left." Matthew ch.25 v32-33

Rewards in the kingdom of heaven are given to those who serve without any thought of reward. There is no hint of merit here for God gives only to those who work for him. He will separate the ones before the judgement, like sheep and like goats. He will put his right hand only on the sheep to protect and care for them. It is important that 'working for Jesus' is not going out preaching or teaching to the lost. If the person is a slave, or has illness, or is in prison, the Holy Spirit will show you what you have to do. But the 'fruit' will still be there.

Jesus said, "Thus by their fruit you will recognise them." Matthew ch.7 v20

God sends his sun and rain on the good and the bad, he doesn't separate them. The evil persons have not realised that God is his wisdom on earth has made it a place to live. Not like the planets that go round the sun or even Pluto or Jupiter. He sends the weather to make it a home for us to stay.

- - - - - - - -

Jesus said, "That your giving may be in secret. Then your Father, who sees what is done is secret, will reward you." Matthew ch.6 v4

This verse indicates a righteousness for giving or gains. Wealth is to be used and not stored away, it is a process of giving away what you have over. When you are dead, what will happen to the riches that you have gained? What fortune have you made for yourself? It will be lost as your descendants will waste it away.

Goods

Goods are having suitable or desirable qualities, promoting health, welfare or happiness.

Now the valley of Siddim was full of tar pits, and when the kings of Sodom and Gomorrah fled, some of the men fell into them and the rest fled to the hills. The four kings seized all their gods of Sodom and Gomorrah and all their food; then they went away. Genesis ch.14 v10-11

Lumps of asphalt are often seen today floating in the southern end of the Dead Sea. The tar pits were recorded in the Bible. The lowest body of water on earth and is flanked by hills on both sides. Lot decided to go into Sodom as a town, he was living among the unrighteous people (see 2 Peter ch.2 v7-8).

Abram recovered all the goods that had been taken, and he brought back his nephew Lot with his possessions and all the women and other captives. Genesis ch.14 v16 (NLT)

All Lot's goods, the four kings took it all away, the food and the women were taken. But Abraham recovered all the goods that had gone, but Abraham and Lot were related he was Abraham nephew.

- - - - - - - -

If a man gives his neighbour silver or goods for safekeeping and they are stolen from the neighbour's house, the thief, if he is caught, must pay back double. But if the thief is not found, the owner of the house must appear before the judges to determine whether he has laid his hands on the other man's property ... the one whom the judges declare guilty must pay back double to his neighbour. Exodus ch.22 v7-9

The judges were God's representatives in court cases, they would decide who was to blame. If one gave his silver or goods to another and if a thief decided to take what was not his own, the thief or the neighbour has to pay back double the quantity. It gave each man what he had, it would be God's way of avoiding having to pay back more than the property. You would have to guard it properly otherwise you will pay back double for the goods.

It was true that even Zacchaeus the tax collector, in the New Testament had to give back four times more than he stole (see Luke ch.19 v8). He even went further than that.

- - - - - - - -

Their treasures will be thrown into deepest darkness. A wildfire will devour their goods, consuming all they have left. Job ch.20 v26 (NLT)

Zophar the Naamathite said to Job, 'My troubled thoughts prompt me to answer'. He said that, 'A wildfire will devour their goods'. Zophar was trying to reply to Job's question, why did God punish him? The word 'treasures' will indicate that all of Job possessions will be forfeit if he upsets God. God is not like that, he sends the sun and rain even on the guilty party or the wicked. He protects all of the natural existence even the mountain goats when they give birth. The mountain goats are high up in the hills avoiding even man, they scatter when man approaches, but God keep watch over them (see Job ch.39 v1).

In all this, Job did not sin by charging God with wrongdoing. Job ch.1 v22

Job's family had been completely destroyed (see Job ch.1 v13-19). By Satan to try to make him blame God, but Job didn't do it. Zophar was pleading with Job for all his treasures and goods were gone, but Job maintained his innocence. When the three friends heard about Job, they could hardly recognise him, they began to weep aloud and tear their clothes. They saw how great his suffering was (see Job ch.2 v11-13). Job gave his children away and his servants, but still Satan attacked him with boils all over his body, even his wife didn't understand. The goods were meaningless for Job. He wanted his life to be spared. He even took a piece of broken pottery to scrape himself (see Job ch.2 v8), the goods were meaningless to him.

The Lord accepted Job's prayer and made him prosperous again and gave him twice as much as he had before (see Job ch.42 v10).

- - - - - - - -

Have you come to plunder? Have you gathered your hordes to loot, to carry of silver and gold, to take away the livestock and goods and to seize much plunder? Ezekiel ch.38 v13

Ezekiel was a priest (see Ezekiel ch.1 v3) and he was taken away by King Nebuchadnezzar of Babylon (see 2 Kings ch.24 v14). Ezekiel was called to minister to the exiles of Judah, his message was with the temple in Jerusalem. He said, 'The goods were to be taken by the Babylonians' (see Ezekiel ch.24 v2, v14).

He also referred to a number of nations in which he had a prophecy about Gog in the land of Magog. The word of the Lord came to him and he spoke about the desolation of the world powers to destroy God's kingdom (see Ezekiel ch.38 - ch.39).

Get ready, be prepared, you and all the hordes around you, and take command of them. After many days you will be called to arms. Ezekiel ch.38 v7-8

Have you come to plunder? Taking away the Israelites who were living in safety (see Ezekiel ch.38 v14); God will act against the hordes of people. Then they will know 'that I am the Lord' (see Ezekiel ch.38 v23).

- - - - - - - -

"Teach the law to anyone who does not know it. Anyone who refuses to obey the law of your God and the law of the king will be punished immediately, either by death, banishment, confiscation of goods, or imprisonment." Ezra ch.7 v25-26 (NLT)

When the exile was finally over. King Artaxerxes gave Ezra the priest, a teacher of the 'Law of the God of heaven' (see Ezra ch.7 v12). He sent Ezra down to Jerusalem to give honour to the Lord's house in this way. The Lord who has extended his good favour to the king and his advisors and powerful officials. 'Teach the Law to whoever doesn't know it'. By taking away all his goods, or even death. It was an important job for Ezra to do. He stood on a high wooden platform, built for this occasion to read it aloud from daybreak till noon. As he faced the men, women and others who could understand. All the people listened attentively to the Book of the Law of Moses (see Nehemiah ch.8 v1-6).

Ezra read from the Law of God and the people acknowledged that he had come from the king of Medes to obey what Ezra said to them.

- - - - - - - -

Then he said, "This is what I'll do. I will tear down my barns and build bigger ones, and there I will store all my grain and my goods. Luke ch.12 v18

Jesus taught the parable of the Rich Fool. A certain rich man produces a good crop, he said, What shall I do, 'I have achieved more than I could want? This is more than all my barns have stored, much more.' God said to him, 'This night your very life will be demanded of you, then who will get what you have prepared for yourself?' When we go out to work and have plenty of money, more than we need. We can eat, drink and life is easy than when we had nothing. We have forgotten the words that we are strangers here, we will come and go and life will go on.

It is important that we don't think of money as a tool, we should be looking first at God's kingdom and his righteousness (see Matthew ch.6 v33). Jesus wanted us to prepare for his kingdom. Not to waste time thinking about all of his goods.

- - - - - - - -

The merchants of the world will weep and mourn for her, for there is no one left to buy their goods. She bought great quantities of gold, silver, jewels, and pearls; fine linen, purple, silk, and scarlet cloth; things made of fragrant thyine wood, ivory goods, and objects made of expensive wood; and bronze, iron, and marble. She also bought cinnamon, spice, incense, myrrh, frankincense, wine, olive oil, fine flour, wheat, cattle, sheep, horses, chariots, and bodies—that is, human slaves. Revelation ch.18 v11-13 (NLT)

What we will do with all our profits? Everything that we had and that is goods for us:

Metals - gold, silver, bronze, iron and marble.

Precious objects - jewels and pearls.

Fine linen - purple, silk and scarlet cloth.

Wood - fragrant thyine.

Ivory that came from dead animals.

Spices - cinnamon, incense, myrrh and frankincense.

Products - wine, olive oil and wheat.

Cattle - sheep, horses.

Bodies - chariots and human slaves.

The merchants, terrified at the earth's torment they see the smoke of her burning and they will weep over her (see Revelation ch.18). Such great wealth has been brought to ruin. With great violence the city will be thrown down, never to be found again. What will happen to all the goods? This is the end, this is the final event and no more profit that we can make on this earth. No workman of any trade will ever be found in you again, the light of a lamp will never shine in you again, the voice of bridegroom and bride will never be heard in you again.

This is the moment that we will be faced with the judgement, the hour that God has planned from the very beginning when the people sinned. The goods will be finished.

Harvest

Harvest as the time of gathering in crops, fruits or the product of result of any labour or act.

"Never again will I destroy all living creatures, as I have done. As long as the earth remains, there will be planting and harvest, cold and heat, summer and winter, day and night." Genesis ch.8 v21-22 (NLT)

God flooded the earth because of man's sin and wickedness, he intended to remove all of the violence that the earth had provided. He even destroyed all of the animals, the birds and the plants. It lasted on earth for one hundred and fifty days (see Genesis ch.7 v24). He provided an ark in which only eight people, several animals and birds were there in the ark to float above the waters. Each animal and bird according to its kind (see Genesis ch.1 v26). God didn't want to start again.

After the flood, God said, 'As long as the earth remains there will be harvest, whatever the weather.'

- - - - - - - -

Celebrate the Feast of Harvest with the firstfruits of the crops you sow in your field. Exodus ch.23 v16

When Israel moved out of Egypt while they were indeed slaves, ill-treated with bricks and work in the fields, slave masters over them to keep them working. They arrived at the mountain of God, Mount Sinai where the Lord had reminded Moses and said, 'Celebrate the Feast of Harvest'. They took seeds from the Egyptians and did as God commanded them. The crops you will sow in the Promised Land to make a harvest of blessing. The crops will grow and you will become richer.

Over many centuries with the kings who were bad and evil, because the Israelites failed to do as God instructed. They treated idols as gods and they were taken way as slaves by the Assyrian and Babylonian empires. The harvest was not to them, but the empires had it all (see Lamentations ch.1 v11).

- - - - - - - -

So Ruth worked alongside the women in Boaz's fields and gathered grain with them until the end of the barley harvest. Then she continued working with them through the wheat harvest in early summer. Ruth ch.2 v23 (NLT)

Ruth was a Moabitess an outsider, one who can be separated from the Israelites. She came back with Naomi to Bethlehem because there was a famine in the land of Israel. Ruth was a selfless devotion to her mother-in-law and the story is set in the time of the Judges, before the kings. Ruth worked hard and she went out reaping in the fields. Gathering grain left behind the servant girls who collected it up after the men had cut the grains with either a scythe or a sickle. It was the poor girl who was the last in line with the harvest, collecting what had been left for her to find.

The barley harvest was a lot of work taking an amount of bending over to gather. She gleaned in the field and produced an ephah of barley (the ephah was a large container holding about twenty-two litres). The amount of barley was small and could be threshed by hand simply by beating it with a club or stick. Ruth had collected about half a hundred weight of barley. There is a lot of barley to be collected by the poor and the widow provided they go out into the harvest and collected what the owners didn't want, or left behind (see Leviticus ch.19 v9-10).

- - - - - - - -

You take care of the earth and water it, making it rich and fertile. The river of God has plenty of water; it provides a bountiful harvest of grain, for you have ordered it so. Psalm ch.65 v9 (NLT)

We can sow the seed for grain but God has to water it. Making the soil rich and fertile because God had planned it so after the flood with Noah. The soil needs water not drenching it with rain, but slowly over time. The beetles and worms like the soft ground and they aerate it properly. The soil sits there, waiting for the rain to come, every week the rain falls on the ground and God is patient and gives us rain when we need it.

The harvest needs sun and rain as well as seed.

- - - - - - - -

Now this is what the Lord Almighty says: "Give careful thought to your ways.

You have planted much, but have harvested little." Haggai ch.1 v5

After the people went back to the Promised Land, they had returned to their property. Building their houses once again, planting seed, going out with their friends. God Almighty says, 'Think what you want out of life. I waited for you to build your houses, but you have forgotten my house, my temple. Which has been ruined by the Babylonians, burnt down to the ground. I was patient, but now my house needs attention. You have planted seed, but you never have enough.'

So the Lord stirred up Zerubbabel governor of Judah, Joshua the high priest and the whole remnant of the people:

They came and began work on the house of the Lord Almighty, their God. Haggai ch.1 v14

They worked on the temple of the Lord, sacrificing what they had been doing in the fields, but God remembered their sacrifice and gave them plenty of food to eat.

- - - - - - - -

Do not be deceived: God cannot be mocked. A man reaps what he sows. The one who sows to please his sinful nature, from that nature will reap destruction; the one who sows to please the Spirit, from the Spirit will reap eternal life. Galatians ch.6 v7-8

Don't think that God is to be made fun of, to be laughed at, or mocked: a man reaps what he sows, to please his sinful nature and it results in destruction. A man sows what pleases the Holy Spirit and it will give eternal life. This is the difference a harvest makes.

Each man has his own way of doing things, some sow, but others harvest and reap. Remember what God is saying to you. Harvest what is from the Holy Spirit and you will reap from what is above, to enter the kingdom of God. Regardless of the multitude of friends and books around you, sow the harvest correctly and you will find that you will have more left over.

Home

Home as a dwelling place and the residence of one's one family, the scene of domestic life.

The victorious invaders then plundered Sodom and Gomorrah and headed for home, taking with them all the spoils of war and the food supplies.   Genesis ch.14 v11 (NLT)

In the time of Abraham, the four kings carried off Lot (his nephew) who was staying on Sodom and all his possessions, even the food. Abraham called out his 318 trained men and pursued them as far as Dan (see Genesis ch.14 v14). He recovered all the goods and brought them back together with the women and the other people (see Genesis ch.14 v16). He did not ask for anything. Not even a thread, or a thong of a sandal (see Genesis ch.14 v23-24). They went home with nothing but what my men have eaten and the share that belongs to my men.

Lot had been rescued.

- - - - - - - -

Jacob said to Laban, "Please release me so I can go home to my own country. Let me take my wives and children, for I have earned them by serving you, and let me be on my way. You certainly know how hard I have worked for you." Genesis ch.30 v25-26 (NLT)

Jacob worked for Laban for seven years for his youngest daughter. But when the marriage came, he was passed over for the other eldest daughter who had 'weak eyes'. So he decided to work for fourteen years for the both of them (see Genesis ch.29 v16-18, v26-27).

Laban tricked Jacob to work for him shepherding his sheep. He would be out all night long keeping the sheep protected from lions and bears (see 1 Samuel ch.17 v34-35). But he deceived Laban by taking the speckled and spotted sheep away from him, he did it by placing the white stripes in the feeding trough when the stronger animals were in heat (see Genesis ch.30 v43). He wanted to go back to his family his home. Or, because Laban tricked him and changed his wages several times, he thought that he could be even (see Genesis ch.31 v17-19).

- - - - - - - -

If a man has recently married, he must not be sent to war or have any other duty placed on him. For one year he is to be free to stay at home and bring happiness to the wife he has married. Deuteronomy ch.24 v5

In the Mosaic law every man who has married will not be taking any duties at all. Not going away to fight for he might be killed. For one year he must be at home, he loved his mistress and wanted to be close to her.

This is the way to get the inheritance of the tribes secured. The home is where the heart is. The Israelites understood that the duties of a married man to see that his children were assured and that he had to be there. This is why there is a lot of counting of their relatives, it really mattered to them (see 1 Chronicles ch.1 - ch.8).

The grave is their eternal home, where they will stay forever. They may name their estates after themselves, but their fame will not last. They will die, just like animals. Psalm ch.49 v11-12 (NLT)

Otherwise, they would eventually die and the grave is their 'eternal home'. It is a reference to Sheol the place of the dead. The tribes would remain as one together. If one came down from Syria and approached Asher, or if one came up from Egypt went after Simeon, or if the Philistines were attacking Judah or the plains in Gilead from north or south. Then the whole tribes would unite and fight off the enemy. This is a successful unity of men they could all fight together.

As an example: the inheritance in Israel would come together to fight against Benjamin (see Judges ch.20 v46-48), because a Levite and his concubine had a nasty experience in Gibeah (see Judges ch.19 v22-26).

The people grieved for Benjamin, because the Lord had made a gap in the tribes of Israel. Judges ch.21 v15

One tribe had almost been wiped out. The men of Israel had taken an oath: 'Not one of us will give his daughter in marriage to a Benjamite'. One of those from Jabesh Gilead had not attended the meeting, but there was an annual festival of the Lord in Shiloh (see Judges ch.21 v8-9). So they instructed the tribe of Benjamin to go and find wives for them to reconstruct the whole fighting force.

- - - - - - - -

Another of his disciples said, "Lord, first let me return home and bury my father." Jesus told him, "Follow me now. Let the spiritually dead bury their own dead." Matthew ch.8 v21-22 (NLT)

One of his disciples had a father who had died. But Jesus corrected him. Why?

Jesus told the disciple to follow him:

> The burial would take a long while.

> The duties of his son to take care of his mother.

> If the disciple was the only son he had.

> He might have looked and provided for his family.

The time of Jesus ministry was short and demanded full attention and commitment. This indicates that the demands of Jesus discipleship; since Jews have placed great importance on the duty of children to bury their parents.

Spiritually Dead: everyone must die because the sin was there from the moment the child was born. It was a relationship from Adam (see Romans ch.5 v12). The moment we die we are lost and spiritually dead from God (see Romans ch.8 v7-8). We are not going to heaven where God is. The only way we can get to heaven is by believing on Jesus who is our Lord and Saviour (see Romans ch.8 v12-14).

This was the mission of Jesus and he only lasted a short time on this earth.

- - - - - - - -

Even now we go hungry and thirsty, and we don't have enough clothes to keep warm. We are often beaten and have no home. We work wearily with our own hands to earn our living. We bless those who curse us. We are patient with those who abuse us. 1 Corinthians ch.4 v11-12 (NLT)

The apostle Paul indicated that he had worked hard to let the Gentile believers come to the Lord. The devil, who is the master of evil, the unseen power of unbelief and ungodliness had tried to stop him. This is why he was beaten and had no real home. We work wearily with and own hands, which Paul should not have been doing at this stage in his life. The cost of discipleship is really tough if you go out teaching the unbelievers you can be sure that Satan and his fallen angels will follow and pursue you. It is the way for the work of Jesus. He was betrayed, arrested and sent to the Romans who crucified him, but he didn't say anything at all (see Matthew ch.26 v62-63; Mark ch.15 v3-5).

- - - - - - - -

In a wealthy home some utensils are made of gold and silver, and some are made of wood and clay. The expensive utensils are used for special occasions, and the cheap ones are for everyday use. If you keep yourself pure, you will be a special utensil for honourable use. Your life will be clean, and you will be ready for the Master to use you for every good work. 2 Timothy ch.2 v20-21 (NLT)

In a wealthy home some things are made of gold and some are made of wood. Why did the apostle Paul say that?

If you keep yourself pure.

You will be honest, your life will be clean.

You can be ready for Jesus.

To use you for special work.

If you fail to be useful, you can sit at home looking like wood or clay. You might be saved, or you might not. You won't be there looking for the day where the Lord will return again. If you are back in your house you can relax, take it easy, many necessary things will occupy your time. The time will fly by and then when you die, Jesus will ask you what you did?

So the last will be first, and the first will be last. Matthew ch.20 v16

Do you want to own up and that your time was wasted on earth?

- - - - - - - -

For this world is not our permanent home; we are looking forward to a home yet to come. Hebrews ch.13 v14 (NLT)

This world is not ours to enjoy. We are looking forward to a home or a city yet to come. This is why there is not much time to do it, every day goes by so what have we done today? I'm not suggesting that we go out every day. Some things, if you are not well, or have a disability or not being too old or young.

The purpose is that every day we should be like 'salt and light' (see Matthew ch.5 v13-16). What do we mean by that? If the salt loses its saltiness, how can it be made salty again? A city on a hill cannot be hidden, neither do you put a lamp under a bowl. Salt has a real taste and a light shines before men. That's what you have to do and show your good deeds and praise your Father who is in heaven.

Inheritance

Inheritance is to make an heir and to get possession from past generations.

Say to the Israelites, "If a man dies and leaves no son, give his inheritance over to his daughter. If he has no daughter, give his inheritance to his brothers. If he has no brothers, give his inheritance to his father's brothers. If his father had no brothers, give his inheritance to the nearest relative in his clan, that he may possess it. This is a legal requirement for the Israelites, as the Lord commanded Moses." Numbers ch.27 v8-11

God instructed Moses to specify what will happen to a man if he dies. There is lot of fighting when a man dies, particularly if he is wealthy in our country. All the relatives get together, scuffles and even fight for his things. This is not what God wanted for the Israelites. So God commanded what should be done with his inheritance. To keep it within his tribe to differentiate between the clan or family. Otherwise, over the years the separation between the tribes would be lost.

- - - - - - - -

He ordered you to give the inheritance by lot to our brother Zelophehad to his daughters ... Then at the Lord's command Moses gave this order to the Israelites ... They may marry anyone they please as long they marry within the tribal clan of their father. Numbers ch.36 v2, v5-6

What the daughters of Manasseh were saying to Moses, 'If they married without their own tribe, their inheritance will be taken away from them'. So all of the daughters married with in their own clan, each one of them (Mahlah, Tizrah, Hoglah, Milcah and Noah) had an inheritance from Zelophehad. They married cousins on their father's side.

There was a split inheritance between the five sisters. The rights of the firstborn daughter were not considered.

- - - - - - - -

When the man divides his inheritance, he may not give the larger inheritance to his younger son, the son of the wife he loves, as if he were the firstborn son. He must recognize the rights of his oldest son, the son of the wife he does not love, by giving him a double portion. He is the first son of his father's virility, and the rights of the firstborn belong to him. Deuteronomy ch.21 v16-17 (NLT)

Particularly when a man married a woman in his last days, in his old age. He might decide to give his later son to have his inheritance, overriding the other sons and daughters (see Genesis ch.37 v3-4). You can see it from the kings of Israel and Judah. The order of birth rather than parental favouritism governed succession. Though the rule was sometimes set aside with divine approval. Like Jacob or kings David and Solomon.

- - - - - - - -

Here is the fate God allots to the wicked, the heritage a ruthless man receives from the Almighty: However, many his children, their fate is the sword, his offspring will never have enough to eat. The plague will bury those who survive him, and their widows will not weep over them. Job ch.27 v13-15

If a firstborn son was wicked and cruel, Job in his discourse pointed out that his sons after him would all be killed and come to nothing. A person who is honourable, stabilised the family and his sons would be respected and be true to what God has indicated in his instructions. But not the wicked, his sons would be evil like him and eventually come to nothing.

- - - - - - - -

So now, with God as our witness, and in the sight of all Israel—the Lord's assembly—I give you this charge. Be careful to obey all the commands of the Lord your God, so that you may continue to possess this good land and leave it to your children as a permanent inheritance. 1 Chronicles ch.28 v8 (NLT)

David was not the firstborn son, but he ruled Israel with kindness and valour. He was the youngest of his brothers. His father, Jesse had Eliab as the firstborn son (see 1 Samuel ch.16 v1-13).

After Jesse passed away his children became his 'permanent inheritance'. We don't know, because king David had command over Israel who could do what he liked, provided he kept what God had instructed (see 2 Samuel ch.7 v3). When he overcame Goliath, he was presented with wealth from king Saul. In addition, king Saul would exempt his father's family from taxes in Israel and that would help his brothers (1 Samuel ch.17 v25).

Our inheritance has been turned over to aliens, our homes to foreigners. We have become orphans and fatherless, our mothers like widows. We must buy the water we drink; our wood can only be had at a price. Lamentations ch.5 v2-4

When the Babylonians overthrew Jerusalem, they took all of the rest of the people to Babylon, leaving behind the poorest people of the land to work the vineyards and the fields (see 2 Kings ch.25 v11-12). The book of Lamentations describes what the people thought that they were worthless, God didn't like them anymore. Their inheritance was taken away and they had to 'buy water and wood'. I am not surprised the people became bitter because they treated idols and worshipped what the people of the nations around them; they disrespected God and didn't follow his instructions which he had clearly laid out in the Torah (the five books of the Old Testament), and God had sent many prophets but they ignored them.

In the New Testament when Jesus came, the church was indeed different. Jesus' believers were strangers on earth, the inheritance was meaningless. They focussed on the return of Jesus and the eternal life which will be to come.

He overthrew seven nations in Canaan and gave their land to his people as their inheritance. All this took about 450 years. Acts ch.13 v19-20

In the past, God overthrew the nations and gave his people the Promised Land as the Lord's inheritance. God tests us in order to see if our faith is strong or to prove our commitment.

He asked Abraham, to offer his son, Issac whom you love. His only son he was getting old, not to soon to have another son. To offer his son as a sacrifice as a burnt offering. Abraham went and trusted God. As he took the knife to slay his son but God didn't let him do that. He waited until the third day to see if Abraham, he watched until Isaac was bound up and placed on the wood and Abraham reached for his knife. Three days while Abraham considered what he should do. This is why that God gave Abraham his inheritance. It was a sign like God's only son Jesus, but he had to die on his own nailed to a cross.

The inheritance from the father to son didn't matter at all. He trusted God and that was the right thing to do.

- - - - - - - -

And now I entrust you to God and the message of his grace that is able to build you up and give you an inheritance with all those he has set apart for himself. Acts ch.20 v32 (NLT)

God had an inheritance; he was going to give his children the rights forever. To build you up to make you strong with all those he separated apart for himself. It wasn't like a possession, to make you strong for the Lord to do his work. It was a gift from God that we should be heirs of his kingdom.

When Adam and Eve sinned against the Lord everybody should get old and die. This was God's judgement for anybody who sins. God is holy and he would never accept people, however good they are to come to him. The only way he could make atonement for them if they turned to Jesus and asked him to be a Saviour and Lord of their life.

They were indeed children of God and shared his inheritance (see Ephesians ch.2 v19-22).

- - - - - - - -

It is by grace you have been saved. Ephesians ch.2 v5

God deeply loves all of us, but he is holy and requests us to come to faith in Jesus. If a person doesn't want to, or makes an excuse, or thinks about it later that person is not in the kingdom of God. That is why people are not saved, whoever good they may be. It is by grace you have been saved and not even works: however good they may be. We do the works by the Holy Spirit who came into us and helped us to make treasure in heaven (see Romans ch.8 v11).

- - - - - - - -

We have a priceless inheritance—an inheritance that is kept in heaven for you, pure and undefiled, beyond the reach of change and decay. And through your faith, God is protecting you by his power until you receive this salvation, which is ready to be revealed on the last day for all to see. 1 Peter ch.1 v4-5 (NLT)

God offers us his inheritance kept in heaven for us. Priceless, invaluable and treasured for us who come to faith in Jesus. We understand and know that this earthly life will soon be over, whatever inheritance we might receive from our father. We might suffer and die, we might have difficulties living, but we can look forward to this inheritance kept for us in heaven. Which will be revealed in the last day for everyone to see. The ones who didn't trust Jesus will look and see what our inheritance is, everyone will look, and wonder.

Luxury

Luxury is an abundant means of comfort, ease and pleasure, indulgence in costly pleasures. Anything delightful and often expensive to get on this earth.

The wise have wealth and luxury, but fools spend whatever they get. Proverbs ch.21 v20 (NLT)

On this earth there are a lot of people ignoring and forsaking God. For since the creation of the world, the stars that shine brilliantly when it gets dark, the high mountains that are there and the rivers that flow down to the sea the people around us don't think that God made them (see Romans 1 v20). Each person strives to get rich, taking on more things to get wealthy. This is why when you receive taxes you try to avoid paying them and ignore the authorities that set them up. The rich and the poor. Why do you think that there are estate agents in most streets? They want you to move up and get a house where most people think that you are more prosperous than you are.

The wise are not like that (see Matthew ch.6 v25-34).

- - - - - - - -

What sorrow awaits you who lounge in luxury in Jerusalem, and you who feel secure in Samaria! You are famous and popular in Israel, and people go to you for help. Amos ch.6 v1 (NLT)

The prophet Amos stood outside the religious institutions because he was a shepherd and didn't go to college. He was like an ignorant peasant. Amos was to announce God's judgement of Israel because of the nation's religious idolatry and wasteful indulgence. He was critical of the luxury in Jerusalem and he spoke out what was wrong. Israel was politically secure and spiritually complacent. God would soon bring the whole of the Assyrian Empire and the people in Israel would go into exile.

The prophet doesn't go to university or college and he might not be trained to speak but he has God on his side and that's what make the difference.

- - - - - - - -

Jesus said, "No, those who wear expensive clothes and indulge in luxury are in palaces. But what did you go our to see? A prophet? Yes, I tell you, and more than a prophet." Luke ch.7 v25-26

He was talking about John the Baptist who was imprisoned by Herod. Philip's wife Herodias, whom Herod had married. She should not have married Herod (see Mark ch.6 v17-18).

Herodias: a granddaughter of Herod the Great. First, she married her uncle, Herod Philip who lived in Rome. While a guest in their home in Rome, Herod Antipas persuaded Herodias to leave her husband for him. Married to one's brother wife, while he was still around was forbidden by the Mosaic Law (see Leviticus ch.18 v16).

Herodias nursed a grudge against John (the Baptist) and wanted to kill him. But she was not able to. Mark ch.6 v19

John the Baptist wore clothes made of camel's hair and he had a leather belt around his waist. His food was locusts and wild honey (see Matthew ch.3 v4). John's simple food, clothing and lifestyle were a visual protest against self-indulgence. Only a few lived in luxury and they were in palaces.

- - - - - - - -

You have lived on earth in luxury and self-indulgence. You have fattened yourself in the day of slaughter. You have condemned and murdered innocent men, who were not opposing you. James ch.5 v5-6

The book of James was focused on the believers and accompanied by good deeds plus a faith that works. It was written for the 'twelve tribes scattered among the nations' (see James ch.1 v1).

It is written by James the brother of the Lord and it is taking about the rich:

> That you have lived a luxury life on earth.

> That you have been self-indulge, 'fatten yourself' as mankind.

> That you have condemned and murdered innocent men.

Why when they are not opposing you? Your wealth has rotted, moths have eaten your clothes, precious metals are corroded and you have hoarded wealth in the last days (see James ch.5 v1-3). The labourers have cried out to the Lord Almighty and he has heard of what you have done. The wages you promised to pay the workmen you have deliberately not given to them. It is true today when you do a job for a fixed sum of money and the person doesn't pay you. You have to write it off as a lost cause.

Being rich doesn't and have a very nice house, doesn't mean that you have to be nasty and mean. God will be aware of it and when the time comes you will regret doing that to the workers.

- - - - - - - -

Give her as much torture and grief as the glory and luxury she gave herself. In her heart she boasts, "I sit as queen; I am not a widow, and I will never mourn." Revelation ch.18 v7

The Rome was the capital of the empire it was the centre of the world. 'Babylon' was the centre of wealth and it was a beautiful city, the queen of the kingdom. Each nation has a time of wealth and affluence, so what do they do with it? The British Empire established itself as a major world power and the nation was well-positioned to compete with territories of its own. But the riches and wealth that came from this led to many heartaches across the world and it is still going on today.

Fallen is 'Babylon the Great', she has become a haunt for demons. God the Father has finished the time on earth, Jesus is going to come again and fight against the Satan and his fallen angels (see Revelation ch.19 v11-21). After that there is the judgement of the dead. Eventually the time for nations has come to an end, God will decide what will have to be done. Babylon luxury is finished and gone forever. But you did not consider these things and reflect on what might happen? (see Isaiah ch.47 v5-15).

Fruit

Fruit is the produce of the earth. It is the edible part of the plant generally sweet, acid and juicy.

This is a powerful concept. When the tree is flowering and then the fruit is formed. The fruit can't appear on the tree without the sap flowing through the tree. In the New Testament times either the fruit is bad (in Satan), or the fruit is good (in Jesus).

Likewise, every good tree bears good fruit, but a bad tree bears bad fruit. A good tree cannot bear bad fruit, and a bad tree cannot produce good fruit. Every tree that does not bear good fruit is cut down and thrown into the fire. Thus, by their fruit you can recognise them. Matthew ch.7 v17-20

The whole fruit of a bad tree is going into the fire to be burnt. When you die, your soul goes back to God and is waiting in Hades. There is a distinction between those who have accepted Jesus as Saviour and Lord of their lives with those that haven't. It is pictured with Jesus describing the difference between them in The Rich Man and Lazarus parable (see Luke ch.16 v16-31).

Then the judgement will start when Jesus returns back to the earth. It will be a long time and we will all have to wait (see 1 Thessalonians ch.4 v16). When the judgement of God commences, John the apostle saw a great white throne all the dead were gathered before him (see Revelation ch.20 v11-12). Sadly, those who didn't respond to Jesus, he or she was thrown into the lake of fire, being bad and evil fruit. But the parable indicates that suffering and tragedy is part of what man can expect in Hades.

- - - - - - - -

Remain in me, and I will remain with you. No branch can bear good fruit by itself; it must remain in the vine. Neither can you bear fruit unless you remain in me. John ch.15 v4

When we come to Jesus and ask him to be our Saviour and Lord of our life. We will change from following Satan to following God and the sap will flow through and into us. The Holy Spirit will enter our lives and make a difference. It does not mean that we will be good, it takes a long while for the 'old order under Satan' to be removed. If you have bad habits try to control them and it might take several years. This is what sanctification, setting apart is all about.

Sanctification: it teaches us to say 'no' to ungodliness and worldly passions and to live self controlled, upright and godly lives (see Titus ch.2 v12).

- - - - - - - -

Jesus said, "Forgive us our sins, for we also forgive everyone who sins against us." Luke ch.11 v4

Each day we must come to him in prayer and ask for our sins to be forgiven. It is important that we forgive others who sin against us. How can we ask God to forgive us our sins when we have enemies that we hate? (see Matthew ch.6 v14-15). This is an important fact to be taken away, to be reflect upon and ponder over.

We pray this in order that you may live a life worthy of the Lord and may please him in every way: bearing fruit in every good work, growing in the knowledge of God. Colossians ch.1 v10

You may live a thoroughly, good life. Meaning that we wake up and as we go through the day, Jesus will give us pointers and instructions through the Holy Spirit, to guide us in what to do. It's a faint instruction but grows louder as we study the Bible and pray to our majestic God. Gradually over the years it will be stronger and more insistent. The Holy Spirit will gradually help us in what we must fulfil and achieve. This is what we mean by 'growing in the knowledge of God'. It takes time.

'Good fruit' is what Jesus wants us to carry out. We are left here for a purpose: we are forbearing to everyone; forgiving each person who sins against us. This is the sort of person we should be. Not thinking about riches or assets or wealth because that it is not the way that we should tread this path.

- - - - - - - -

Jesus said, "Everyone who has left houses or brothers or sisters or father or mother or children of fields for my sake will receive a hundred times as much as will inherit eternal life" Matthew ch.19 v29

The way forward is often going against people's and church's tradition. Sadly, we must go forward, even if it means leaving our house with all its security. It is not the easiest path to pursue at all. This is what is means. 'Everyone who has left what is the right kind of fellowship for my sake' will get a reward from Jesus who knows what we mean to him.

The route is often rugged and narrow and the path seems so often overgrown (see Matthew ch.7 v11-14). We go on confidently and purposely, happy that we are tread the pathway to eternal life, but only a few find it. Most people favour the road that leads downhill, it is an easy task. Look at the prophets in the Old Testament, what did they do? They spoke the words of the Lord regardless of the consequences.

Consider the prophet Amos: 'God said I hate your religious feasts ... away with the noise of your songs' (see Amos ch.5 v21, v23).

No wonder, God said, 'Your songs and your feasts I can't stand!' They didn't realise that social justice and true piety means that God will respond to the people rather than singing and feasts. Do you think that Amos was upset? Or go back to Judah? Carrying on with his prophetic ministry.

- - - - - - - - -

God does not show favouritism. Romans ch.2 v11

God will judge what is right whether good or bad. Each one may receive what is due to him for the things done in the body while here on earth and not in Sheol or Hades (2 Corinthians ch.5 v10). There is no injustice, no preference, nothing that we can produce that will sway God to let us off. No money we could bribe God, when we die there is nothing we could take with us. We are there with all the others who face God. We can respond to him and he will answer you (see Matthew ch.25 v44-45). There will be rewards and crowns.

There is no distinction between the rights of the rich and the poor, the slave and the free. Everyone should be waiting to hear what God will say to them it is contained by the books that specify the time we were born until the time we die (see Revelation ch.20 v12). Hidden and secret things which God has noted down in his books.

Loan

Loan is the act of lending to have an arrangement for permission to use it for your own good.

If you take your neighbour's cloak as security for a loan, you must return it before sunset. This coat may be the only blanket your neighbour has. How can a person sleep without it? If you do not return it and your neighbour cries out to me for help, then I will hear, for I am merciful. Exodus ch.22 v26-27 (NLT)

The poor, the widow, the orphan, the alien in fact, all defenceless people and objects of God's special concern and providential care. Anyone who thinks that man or woman doesn't really matter. Who cares if they don't have a coat? We desperately need and want the money. When they cry out to God for help and the Lord will hear and respond kindly.

Jesus said: (see Matthew ch.25 v35-36)

I was hungry you gave me something to eat.

I was thirsty you gave me something to drink.

I was a stranger and you invited me in.

I needed clothes and you clothed me.

I was sick and you looked after me.

I was in prison and you came to visit me.

He will reply, "I tell you the truth, whatever you did not do for one of the least of these, you did not do (it) for me." Matthew ch.25 v45

- - - - - - - -

Do not be mean-spirited and refuse someone a loan because the year for cancelling debts is close at hand. If you refuse to make the loan and the needy person cries out to the Lord, you will be considered guilty of sin. Give generously to the poor, not grudgingly, for the Lord your God will bless you in everything you do. There will always be some in the land who are poor. That is why I am commanding you to share freely with the poor and with other Israelites in need. Deuteronomy ch.15 v9-11 (NLT)

When the time for the Jubilee Year was approaching if one had something that another asked for it, it doesn't really matter you can lend it and God will bless you for it. There will be always be the poor in the Promised Land, it is important that you share what you have. Not, when the time came up for the Jubilee Year.

Therefore, I command you to be open-handed towards your brothers and towards the poor and needy in your land. Deuteronomy ch15 v11

Give generously and not grudgingly to the poor. We are all brother's together: one will be rich and the other will be poor.

- - - - - - - -

Do not charge your brother interest, whether on money or food or anything else that may earn interest. Deuteronomy ch.23 v19

Interest for profit was not intended to be charged at the expense of the poor. It is the same interest for profit as the widow, the orphan, the alien and they couldn't afford the rate of return. This was the Law of Moses which God had provided under the Mount Sinai where Moses went up to meet God. So Moses went back to and summoned the leaders of the people and set before them the words of the Lord God. The people said, "We will do everything the Lord has said" (see Exodus ch.19 v7-8).

It was a reminder to not charge for anything else if one wanted to borrow something of yours.

- - - - - - - -

The wicked snatch a widow's child from her breast, taking the baby as security for a loan. The poor must go about naked, without any clothing. They harvest food for others while they themselves are starving. Job ch.24 v9-10

It's a great pity that the Israelites rejected and ignored the Law of Moses. The people turned down or refused because they wanted more money. They didn't have enough produce or sheep while they were in the Promised Land. All of the buildings were there, they had fields to grow crops, they had trees which were covered with fruit.

But the Israelite were greedy for more:

The wicked snatch a baby from a widow's breast.

The poor must go around naked.

Without any clothing at all.

They are starving without any food.

Yet they suffer thirst.

All for a loan from their brothers.

- - - - - - - -

Later after many years, when the Israelites in Jerusalem considered that the Babylonian empire were surrounding the city, times were hard but the walls were thick and strong. For a time, the Babylonians remained outside the walls, the city had become so severe that there was no food for the people to eat (see 2 Kings ch.25 v1-3).

Then the city wall was broken through, and the whole army fled at night through the gate between the two walls near the king's garden, though the Babylonians were surrounding the city. 2 Kings ch.25 v4.

The army was ready to act at once provided the wall was knocked down, probably at night and the soldiers slipped though the gate. They knew the people were left behind at the mercy of the Babylonians who were there for some while. Waiting for the chance to enter the city to loot and destroy everything. No-one could give any bread to anyone else. They didn't have much to lend out but they had buildings.

- - - - - - - -

Jesus said, "But love your enemies, do good to them, and lend to them without expecting to get anything back. Then your reward will be great, and you will be sons of the Most High, because he is kind to the ungrateful and wicked. Be merciful, just as your Father is merciful." Luke ch.6 v35-36

Generosity in dealing with a loan was extended much further by Jesus. Who taught that lending without receiving anything back was a special thing for God to notice and reward? The Lord is kind to those who need something to borrow. Everyday, the sun comes up and shines for the good and the bad, regardless of what the sinful man is doing. It is the same with the rain, they water the plants where man doesn't go.

God is merciful and we believers should be just like him.

~*Means*

Means to have in mind what is significant to intend, to purpose or to design.

Like a partridge that hatches eggs it did not lay is the man who gains riches by unjust means. When his life is half gone, they will desert him, and in the end he will prove to be a fool. Jeremiah ch.17 v11

Why did the man gain riches by unjust means? The individual was taking what was not his own. They couldn't do anything to stop him. But it was totally wasted as his life was nearly over. In the end he will be a dimwit and an idiot who thought that it didn't matter. Better to do nothing than taking by unjust means. When your life is over, then all of your gains and means will be left on earth. You can't take anything with you and the soul returns to God who created you. Then, there is the judgement where each person has to be reminded of what things they have done on the earth. Whether it is good or bad.

God would point out to the person that he was a fool (see Romans ch.1 v22).

- - - - - - - -

Many will be purified, cleansed, and refined by these trials. But the wicked will continue in their wickedness, and none of them will understand. Only those who are wise will know what it means. Daniel ch.12 v10 (NLT)

Many will fall to the wickedness and be slaves to Satan. Doing the things that they want only to please themselves. If you don't get it; you want it. Like alcohol, like drugs or like sex. The wicked will not understand, the mind of sinful man is death, hostile to God. It does not submit to God's laws, nor can it do so.

Those controlled by the sinful nature cannot please God. Romans ch.8 v8

Whereas the prophet Daniel was talking about the end times where God will protect his people. Not when the remnant of Judah were still in exile, but it will be much later when 'it will be for a time, times and half a time' (see

Daniel ch.12 v7). He heard, but he didn't understand. How could he know? The reign of Jesus will come to pass after 500 years when Daniel received this warning.

When Jesus will come back again and the judgement will come upon us.

- - - - - - - -

For to me, to live is Christ and to die is gain. Philippians ch.1 v21

The apostle Paul remarked about what he was prepared to do to win the Gentiles over to Jesus Christ (see 2 Corinthians ch.11 v23-28). He would feel pressure for all the Gentile churches in Asia Minor, Egypt, Cyprus, Crete and Greece. It was too much to bear. He had helpers, but he was left on his own to care for the churches. This was why he wrote several letters to encourage his disciples, warning them not to fall under the spell of false teachers and false prophets. Eventually, he was falsely imprisoned by the Jews for taking Greeks into the holy temple at Jerusalem.

'For me to life is Christ but to die is gain' he was referring to his time in Philippi. He met a slave girl who told the future who worried and distressed the apostle Paul (see Acts ch.16 v16-18). The crowd joined in on the attack of Paul and Silas, they had been severely flogged and were thrown into prison. To die is to be released from the worries of this life on earth to go and see Jesus. The 'means' were too much to bear.

- - - - - - - -

In his kindness God called you to share in his eternal glory by means of Christ Jesus. So after you have suffered a little while, he will restore, support, and strengthen you, and he will place you on a firm foundation. 1 Peter ch.5 v10 (NLT)

The kindness of God who called you to share in his goodness. He would restore you, support you and strengthen you. Jesus in heaven did not leave his people behind to face persecution and suffering. When you suffer, Jesus would suffer with you. When you are beaten, Jesus would share his pain with you. This is why he will restore you and place you on a 'firm foundation'.

Whatever happens to you as a believer, you can be sure that when the time comes the Holy Spirit will support you and comfort you.

Jesus said, "Do not let your hearts be troubled and do not be afraid." John ch.14 v27

Jesus said, 'Do not let your hearts be troubled'.

"Then you will be handed over to be persecuted and put to death, and you will be hated by all nations because of me." Matthew ch.24 v9

The earth will have good and bad intentions. The bad intentions that the world will be subject to Satan's merciless purpose to dispose of the church and what it stands for. The good intentions are the way to let many believers share what Jesus did to rescue us. He sacrificed his body to his tormentors and gave himself up for us.

Money - The Old Testament

Money is stamped or pressed metal used as a trading mechanism any currency used in the same way.

If you lend money to one of my people among you who is needy, do not be like a money-lender; charge him no interest. Exodus ch.22 v25

When God spoke to Moses at the Mount of Sinai he is referred basically to money. There's a lot of money used in the Old Testament. People doing business with each other, to buy and sell products and this was used as a currency. However, the Lord instructed them not to charge interest between the Israelites. No people of God can charge more than the worth of the item to another Israelite. If you want to be a money-lender you will have to do it outside with the nations around you.

God said, "Charge him no interest." Nothing to add to the poor Israelite people coming to you to buy something. Don't think that you have a spare set of scales, to cheat the person. It is mentioned three times in the book of Proverbs (see Proverbs ch.11 v1, ch.16 v11, ch.20 v23). That is basically wrong and it means inaccurate weights. Silver was weighed on scales balanced against a stone weight. Weights with dishonest labels were used for cheating.

- - - - - - - -

At the end of every seventh year, you must cancel the debts of everyone who owes you money. This is how it must be done. Everyone must cancel the loans they have made to their fellow Israelites. Deuteronomy ch.15 v1-2 (NLT)

Of the seventh year you must not owe money to anyone provided they were Israelites. In the whole of the Promised Land of Israel you cannot owe money. You may require a payment from a foreigner (see Deuteronomy ch.15 v3), but you will give the poor freedom; a chance to release from the money owed to another brother in Israel. So in a measure, a way to equalise wealth. Even in the best of societies under the most enlightened laws, the uncertainties of life, the variations among peoples, result in some people becoming poor. In such cases the Lord commands that generosity and kindness be extended to them.

Since every field was to lie fallow in the Promised Land during the seventh year, because of the Lord's requirement for obedience (see Exodus ch.23 v11). If Israel didn't follow the Lord commands, the reverse would come true (see Deuteronomy ch.28 v43-44). You will sink lower and lower. He will lend to you but you will not lend to him.

- - - - - - - -

Have I put my trust in money or felt secure because of my gold? Have I gloated about my wealth and all that I own? Job ch.31 v24-25 (NLT)

Job was very depressed. He had lost everything, his family, his animals, his slaves and even his house (see Job ch.1 v13-19). Because Satan tried to make him curse God and die, but Job wouldn't (see Job ch.1 v21-22), even his wife blamed God (see Job ch.2 v9). So his three friends Eliphaz, Bildad and Zophar came round to comfort him. They blamed him for displeasing God, but he was obstinate and inflexible, he knew he was right.

Each friend presented their arguments and Job replied, but the friends couldn't make him change his mind. Job said, 'Have I trusted in money, gold and wealth? Will that save me from the trouble'? When the storm came later and God answered Job. He commended Job, but his three friends they presented arguments that were not correct, they were false.

After Job had prayed for his friends, the Lord made him prosperous again and gave him twice as much as he had before. Job ch.42 v10

He had to go through the pain in his illness to gain God's commendation.

- - - - - - - -

Then all of your surviving family will bow before him, begging for money and food. "Please," they will say, "Give us jobs among the priests so we will have enough to eat." 1 Samuel ch.2 v36 (NLT)

Eli the priest had two sons who were very wicked. But they still had control over the temple of the Lord at Shiloh. Because the temple in Jerusalem had not been built by king Solomon. Now a man of God came to Eli and said, 'Why do you scorn my sacrifice and offerings, why do you honour your sons more than me' (see 1 Samuel ch.2 v27-29).

They will be a sign for you - they will both die on the same day. 1 Samuel ch.2 v34

God will raise up a faithful priest. The quiet boy Samuel ministered before the Lord under Eli; he was there in the temple a young man looking to help with the service.

The Lord was with Samuel as he grew up, and he let none of his words fall to the ground. All Israel from Dan to Beersheba recognised that Samuel was attested as a prophet of the Lord. 1 Samuel ch.3 v19-20

God gave Samuel a chance to let none of his words 'fall to the ground'. What that means is none of Samuel words proved unreliable, he spoke the word of the Lord righteously. Faithfully as he grew up, he was dependable and just (see 1 Samuel ch.12 v3).

- - - - - - - -

As Samuel grew old, he appointed his sons to be judges over Israel. Joel and Abijah, his oldest sons, held court in Beersheba. But they were not like their father, for they were greedy for money. They accepted bribes and perverted justice. 1 Samuel ch.8 v1-3 (NLT)

Samuel was the prophet and priest for the whole of Israel. He recognised that God is his wisdom had been there for the time of the Judges. But he was now old, so he set up his sons as Judges for the people. They were not like Samuel for they were unreliable and wasted money.

Their sins were there for all to see:

> They were impatient for money.

> They accepted bribes.

> They perverted the truth.

So all the elders came together at Ramah where Samuel was, and they said,

"Now appoint a king to lead us, such as all the other nations have." *1 Samuel ch.8 v5*

The appointment caused Samuel great pain so he prayed to the Lord. The Lord told him, 'It is not you they are rejecting, but me'. Samuel knew that this is why for the Law of Moses a king was mentioned (see Deuteronomy ch.17 v14-20). They bypassed the Lord and wanted a king to be like the other nations, they wanted a king to lead them in battle. But God was no use to them and he couldn't be seen to guide them.

- - - - - - - -

Whoever loves money never has enough; whoever loves wealth is never satisfied with his income. Ecclesiastes ch.5 v10

Whoever loves money never has enough. Why? This is partly to do with:

We want even more money than other people have got.

We want to go out to the shops and buy things.

We noticed the advertisements from other people's things.

We don't want to be less then other people.

We need more savings in the bank to be safe.

We want added possessions and jewels.

We have holidays, parties going out to be seen.

We dress up to go out and advertising is all around us.

We find taxes annoying and find ways to stop them.

We have energy, fuel, food and clothing to buy.

Everything is woefully expensive and we must get more income.

A party gives laughter, wine gives happiness, and money gives everything! Ecclesiastes ch.10 v19 (NLT)

King Solomon found that money gave us protection and he had more than enough (see 1 Kings ch.10 v14-29). A party is happiness but not really, we eat and drink and have a good time. The party is meaningless unless God is in control.

King Solomon was greater in riches and wisdom than all the other kings of the earth. 1 Kings ch.10 v23

He had a lot of gold, they were symbols of his wealth and glory, he had two hundred shields made of gold. He had a throne built for him and all king Solomon's goblets and articles were made of gold. The king had a fleet of trading ships that came every three years filled with commodities. Year after year the whole world brought gifts to hear his wisdom. He had several hundred chariots and horses (see 2 Chronicles ch.1 v14). King Solomon made silver as common in Jerusalem as stones (see 1 Kings ch.10 v27).

King Solomon wanted more money. He did not release that what God desired for him that he should listen to the words of the Lord, he forgot the passage for him to read every day (see Deuteronomy ch.17 v14-20). It is so hard to be rich and have a communion with God. He fell from God presence, whereas all his money and wealth came to nothing (1 Kings ch.11 v9-11).

- - - - - - - -

Let every priest receive the money from one of the treasurers, and let it be used to repair whatever damage is found in the temple. 2 Kings ch.12 v5

Much later, when Joash was a good king and had Jehoiada the priest instructed him on what he should think and do, but he was only 7 years old (see 2 Kings ch.11 v21). King Joash renews the temple of the Lord and he removed all the Baal and Asherah idols. He burned them outside Jerusalem and all the shrines that his forefathers had constructed, he slaughtered all their false priests. King Joash prepared the Lord's temple which was ruined. After the priest Jehoiada died at the age of a hundred and thirty, king Joash abandoned the temple of the Lord and killed Jehoiada's son (see 2 Chronicles ch.24 v15, v18, v22).

- - - - - - - -

You will eat but never have enough. Your hunger pangs and emptiness will remain. And though you try to save your money, it will come to nothing in the end. Micah ch.6 v14 (NLT)

The prophet Micah's message alternates between doom and hope. The main point of it was the deliverance from God himself. He said, 'It's time you will be ruler over Israel - it was a foretaste of Jesus Christ coming as king over the whole Promised Land (see Micah ch.5 v2). Micah stresses that God hates idolatry, injustice and rebellion. Your 'hunger pangs' will remain. He uses vigorous language and many figures of speech: he tries to influence the Israelites. But without success.

He concludes if you save money, it will come to nothing. Tigath-Pileser III of Assyria led a military campaign in BC 734-732 against Aram, Philistia and parts of Israel and they paid tributes to the king of Assyria. They lost the northern kingdom, most of its territory (see 2 Kings ch.15 v29) and deported the people back to Assyria.

Money is just the root cause of evil, they wanted money so much that they had to be evicted from the land of Israel.

- - - - - - - -

So my people come pretending to be sincere and sit before you. They listen to your words, but they have no intention of doing what you say. Their mouths are full of lustful words, and their hearts seek only after money. Ezekiel ch.33 v31-32 (NLT)

When the people were in exile, both Israel and Judah because they didn't hear or listen to what God wanted them to do. They had idols in various places (see Jeremiah ch.25 v7). They went away from their Promised Land; it had several years rest and solitude. When Ezekiel as a priest said, 'The people you are going to have to settle down and work hard in the country of Babylon'. They wanted to go back to their Promised Land and carry on with what the people had done and even now they wanted to have more idols which the Babylonians had created. God said, 'Your mouths are full of lustful words'. The elders (who should have known better) wanted to look for was more and more money.

Ezekiel was carried away with King Jehoiachin from Jerusalem with about ten thousand men of Judah. He left only the poorest people in the land (see 2 Kings ch.24 v14). The prophet Ezekiel was gifted with a powerful mind and he was capable of grasping the whole scenario of what will happen to the people. He knew that Jerusalem would be destroyed. The Lord removed king Zedekiah to not obey his instructions and commands. Judah went into exile under the Babylonian Empire. Yet all the people were slaves taken away from the Promised Land to go into Babylon for seventy years (see Jeremiah ch.25 v11 and Daniel ch.9 v2).

We belong to the same family as those who are wealthy, and our children are just like theirs. Yet we must sell our children into slavery just to get enough money to live. We have already sold some of our daughters, and we are helpless to do anything about it, for our fields and vineyards are already mortgaged to others. Nehemiah ch.5 v5 (NLT)

The people didn't have enough money:

> We are very poor and not wealthy.

> We must sell our children into slavery.

> We have already sold our daughters.

> We are helpless to do anything about it.

> We have a mortgage on our fields.

Money is not the answer, you have to listen to what God says in the Mosaic Law (see Deuteronomy ch.28).

Money - The New Testament

It is a different matter in the New Testament. Jesus arrived into the earth as a baby, his words and truths made all the difference. Rather than focusing on Israel's bad example he taught that money should be given to the poor. He didn't really have anything of value.

Do not store up for yourself treasures on earth, where moth and rust destroy, and where thieves break in and steal. But store up for yourselves treasures in heaven. Matthew ch.6 v19-20

Jesus pointed out that money must not be used to gain eternal life. Money is there on earth but not in heaven. He said:

Moths destroy treasures, like valuable fabrics.

Rust destroys treasures, like valuable metals.

Thieves break in and take valuable articles.

To steal our treasures like valuable commodities.

Each of us has to decide what to do with the money. Whether we waste it or find opportunities to serve God. Storing up treasures in heaven, what did it mean?

You cannot serve both God and money. Matthew ch.6 v24

Jesus said, 'God and money are really opposite to each other'. If you have one like money, then God is reduced to nothing. If one's serves God, money is reduced to nothing. But he wanted to explain that having money means that you are in an impossible position with the poor looking at you wondering why you don't share with these penniless and impoverished people.

- - - - - - - -

Jesus told him, "If you want to be perfect, go, sell all your possessions and give to the poor, and you will have treasure in heaven. Then come, follow me." Matthew ch.19 v21

Jesus encountered a rich young man, meaning that he was probably a member of an official council or court. The rich man was thinking how he can get to heaven. His way was earning righteousness was to merit eternal life.

Jesus told him:

> 'You want to be perfect.
>
> Go, sell all your possessions.
>
> Give the money to the poor.
>
> Come follow me.'

The rich man was good, the man spoke sincerely because for keeping the law as matter of external conformity. But he had wealth and it removed the obstacle that keeps him from trusting in Jesus. He walked away sadly, but Jesus didn't go after him, neither did he tell his disciples to follow him, he loved him and let him go. The purpose of this is to avoid money and treasures on earth which can get in the way and leave you powerless to aid people. Like, 'You can't serve God and money'.

- - - - - - - -

Then he ordered, "Take the money from this servant, and give it to the one with the ten bags of silver. To those who use well what they are given, even more will be given, and they will have an abundance. But from those who do nothing, even what little they have will be taken away." Matthew ch.25 v28-29 (NLT)

It is the parable of The Talents. A man was going on a long journey. He gave all of his servants and entrusted the money to them. He departed and each of his servants did what was right to them. When he came back each servant had 10, 5, 2 talents. The servant who had 1 talent said, 'You are a hard man so I went out and hid your money in the ground.' The man said to his servant, 'Why did you not give it to the bank and then when I returned I could have it with interest'?

Jesus was going away we don't now when he will be back, it will be a long time. Each servant, like us, had an opportunity to invest his treasure in heaven, but they all had different amounts. Each of us is going about our business and growing up decided not to invest treasure in heaven, but some did. Therefore, the man who buried his money in the ground was taken away to give to those who had more money in heaven. The purpose of the story is to explain that each of us has to have 'treasure in heaven'. If we don't do it the right, all of the work that we will have done will be wasted.

If the servant hid his money, it will be taken away and he will be cast out into the darkness. It is focusing on money because we use it to offer it to the Lord and the poor.

- - - - - - - -

Jesus sat down opposite the place where the offerings were put and watched the crowd putting their money into the temple treasury. Many rich people threw in large amounts. But a poor widow came and put in two very small copper coins, worth only a fraction of a penny ... They all gave out of their wealth; but she, out of her poverty, put in everything - all that she had to live on. Mark ch.12 v41-42, v44

Jesus sat down and watched all the rich people putting their money into the temple treasury and that is a good thing to do. But he noticed a woman who secretly put in everything, all that she had to live on. She was a widow and nobody could help her to fund herself. No holidays, no clothes, no food, no rent, no taxes, nothing.

Located in the court of the women, both men and women were allowed in this court but women could go no further into the temple buildings. It contained thirteen trumpet-shaped receptacles for contributions brought by worshippers.

Jesus said, "I tell you the truth," he said, "this poor widow has put in more than all the others. All these people gave their gifts out of their wealth, but she out of her poverty put in all she had to live on." Luke ch.21 v3-4

The widow brought the smallest copper coins then circulating in Palestine, it was all she had. She gave everything that money could buy.

Then Judas Iscariot, one of the Twelve, went to the chief priests to betray Jesus to them. They were delighted to hear this and promised to give him money. Mark ch.14 v10-11

Contrast that with Judas Iscariot, who decided to betray Jesus to the chief priests for money. It was after Jesus told the parable of the Ten Virgins, parable of The Talents and the parable of The Sheep and the Goats (see Matthew ch.25). Judas did not realise what his master was saying: if we do what he intends he will bless us and give us eternal life. If we do not, he will disown us and punish us.

Money can be used to do dreadful things.

- - - - - - - -

Then some soldiers asked him, "And what should we do?" He replied, "Don't extort money and don't accuse people falsely - be content with your pay." Luke ch.3 v14

John the Baptist was baptising and representing a change in heart, which includes sorrow for sin and a determination to lead a holy life. Some soldiers asked him, 'What should we do?' John replied:

Don't exhort money - like extra money.

Making false accusations - like blaming others.

Be content with your pay - like having enough.

This is what the soldiers were doing. Limited military forces were allowed for certain Jewish leaders and institutions, like the police guard at the temple and escort for military collectors. Be content with your pay. It will badly hurt those eager to get on with more money.

- - - - - - - -

A few days later this younger son packed all his belongings and moved to a distant land, and there he wasted all his money in wild living. About the time his money ran out, a great famine swept over the land, and he began to starve. Luke ch.15 v13-14 (NLT)

Jesus was talking about the parable of The Lost Son. Who went to his father and asked for what was his. The younger son who would not have the firstborn rights and therefore had a limited amount. He made sure when his father was alive, he might get what he thought was his. But the younger son took what was his right, made off with it free from parental restraint. He wasted all his money in 'wild living'. However, he began to starve. Nobody helped him and he was left on his own. He hired himself to the farmer and went into the field to feed pigs. He longed to fill his stomach with the pods that the pigs were eating, for it was a famine over the country where he lived and life was very hard. The ultimate indignity for a Jew; not only was the work distasteful but pigs were unclean animals (see Leviticus ch.11 v7-8)

Lots of money will soon run out and what will you do? There's no income when you are starving in Israel.

- - - - - - - -

The hired hand runs away because he's working only for the money and doesn't really care about the sheep. John ch.10 v13 (NLT)

The hired hand runs away. Why did he run?

> He is only a servant.

> He is only working for the money.

> He doesn't really care for the sheep.

Jesus was talking about the shepherd and his flock. The shepherd goes out day after day and looks after the sheep. He calls the sheep by name. He notices a sheep that was not well. The shepherd opens the door to hold the sheep in during the night. He goes on ahead of them, they know his voice and they will run away from another stranger. If one sheep was lost the shepherd would go after it.

The hired hand is only after the money. He doesn't care for the sheep and he is not interested in what the sheep do. It's only the money that interests him.

- - - - - - - -

All the believers met together in one place and shared everything they had. They sold their property and possessions and shared the money with those in need. Acts ch.2 v44-45 (NLT)

In the early church after Jesus had been raised up from the dead and gone back to heaven. The disciples or apostles had been gathered together and they started the church with the Holy Spirit's help. They did it by sharing the property and possessions with those in need and they also did it also with money.

They started meeting together and distributed what they had. Each one gave what he or she had that is over, not what they had to live on. It is a remarkable thing they did with those in need. Everyone had the same thought by allocating what they didn't require.

- - - - - - - -

Now regarding your question about the money being collected for God's people in Jerusalem. You should follow the same procedure I gave to the churches in Galatia. On the first day of each week, you should each put aside a portion of the money you have earned. 1 Corinthians ch.16 v1-2 (NLT)

In Greece where the Corinthian church was founded. The apostle Paul talked about the collection for the God's people. However, Paul had a strict instruction for what they should be doing. It is the same as giving for God's people. He argued that on the first day of the week a portion of the money should be put aside from what you have earned.

He didn't say how much money you should give. From your earnings you can give what is over what you don't need. It is not like the 'tithe' which requires you to give a tenth to the Lord in the Old Testament (see Numbers ch.18 v25-26).

- - - - - - - -

He must not be a heavy drinker or be violent. He must be gentle, not quarrelsome, and not love money. 1 Timothy ch.3 v3 (NLT)

The apostle Paul said to Timothy on his second missionary journey (see Acts ch.16 v1). The choice of an elder and a deacon must not be a lover of money. He said this to warn the church to avoid going down that path which leads to ruin. Many people have thought that God is love and he is interested in making his believers have riches. It is not so at all.

If the church is led by one who dotes on money he would be sidelined, not being an elder of the church. Riches can make even an elder grasp money and being led astray.

For the love of money is the root of all kinds of evil. And some people, craving money, have wandered from the true faith and pierced themselves with many sorrows. 1 Timothy ch.6 v10 (NLT)

The apostle Paul doesn't do that, he says, 'The love of money is evil'. Many believers think that having money leads to better opportunities. They forget that God created the world and he owns it (see Psalm ch.89 v11).

The Pharisees who loved money and were sneering at Jesus, he was talking about the shrewd manager (Luke ch.16 v14). They wanted money to buy things. Many years later the church and ministers of the churches want money but it is an illusion. You are a believer, you should be focusing on treasures in heaven, you should be thinking about Jesus, he suffered and died for you, he wasn't thinking about money, he didn't have any money at all.

Tell them to use their money to do good. They should be rich in good works and generous to those in need, always being ready to share with others. By doing this they will be storing up their treasure as a good foundation for the future so that they may experience true life. 1 Timothy ch.6 v18-19 (NLT)

The money should be used to do good, being ready to help those in need. This is what the 'treasures in heaven' mean. Give it to the poor who are around you. Not expecting them to reward you, thinking about the poor souls who will always be there (see Matthew ch.26 v11).

- - - - - - - -

Because of these teachers, the way of truth will be slandered. In their greed they will make up clever lies to get hold of your money. But God condemned them long ago, and their destruction will not be delayed. 2 Peter ch.2 v2-3 (NLT)

This is a warning for those who want you to give up your money for the ministers and others to have big houses, big cars, big aeroplanes, big property and so on. They will be motivated by a desire for money and will commercialise the Christian faith to their own selfish advantage.

Although delay makes it seem that they have escaped God's judgement, destruction is going to come upon them. The judgement from God will not pass away and they will be surely accountable. These teachers of the truth are lost souls and will be judged accordingly.

The believers are only interested in the poor to give to the poverty-stricken people the food and security that they need. Not creating ministries and big events.

Possessions

Possessions are means to maintain or control to be master of all events.

Pharaoh ordered some of his men to escort them, and he sent Abram out of the country, along with his wife and all his possessions. Genesis ch.12 v20 (NLT)

There was a famine in the land and Abram went down to Egypt. He did it twice (see Genesis ch.12 and ch.20). Sarai was very beautiful and lovely to look at, but Abram was fearful of the Egyptians mood. Abram said of Sarai his wife, 'She is my sister'. The daughter of my father though not of my mother. Abram's half-truth was a sinful deception, and not a legitimate explanation to the Egyptians.

Abimelech the Pharaoh took her as his wife, but God said in a dream to him, 'You are as good as dead and she is married' (see Genesis ch.20 v3). The Lord had closed up every womb in Abimelech's household, even his slave girls (see Genesis ch.20 v17-18). Then Abram prayed to the Lord so he could be reunited with his wife, he was driven out of Egypt's country with all his possessions.

- - - - - - - -

"But if we do this, all their livestock and possessions will eventually be ours. Come, let's agree to their terms and let them settle here among us." Genesis ch.34 v23 (NLT)

Dinah the daughter of Leah, Jacob wife went out to visit the women of the land. When Shechem the Hivite, saw her he raped her. He said to his father Hamor, "Get me this girl as my wife" (see Genesis ch.34 v1-4).

Jacob's sons became angry that Dinah had been defiled. A thing that should not be done in the land (see Genesis ch.34 v7). Jacob's sons said to the pair of them, 'We can't do that because all of your males are not circumcised' (see Genesis ch.34 v15). So Shechem and Hamor went to talk to the rest of the fellow townsmen and they agreed to carry it out.

They seized their flocks and herds and donkeys and everything else of theirs in the city and out in the fields. *They carried off all their wealth and plunder and all their women and children, taking as plunder everything in the houses.* Genesis ch.34 v28-29

Two of Jacob's sons, Simeon and Levi took their swords and attacked the unsuspecting males, killing every male because they were sore. They plundered the Hivites and took all their possessions.

- - - - - - - -

You will know that your home is safe. When you survey your possessions, nothing will be missing. Job ch.5 v24 (NLT)

Eliphaz is speaking, he is the first one to say that Job was wrong in his thinking. 'If someone venture a word with you, will you not be impatient?' (see Job ch.4 v2). Eliphaz he was convinced as the basics of truth: Your home will be safe. Your possessions will be there. Nothing will be missing. He failed to see that Job's family was devastated and his possession were gone.

His three friends will comfort and reassure Job. He was covered with boils and he sat among the ashes (see Job ch.2 v8). They could hardly recognise him for they saw how great his suffering was (see Job ch.2 v12). What did Job think? It would be better to not have friends like that. All of Job's possessions were gone for Satan had reduced him to nothing, even his children were lost and missing.

- - - - - - - -

I will capture vast amounts of plunder, for the people are rich with livestock and other possessions now. They think the whole world revolves around them!' Ezekiel ch.38 v12 (NLT)

The prophet Ezekiel was pondering about the end times. The time when all the world will have prosperity and comfort. They would not recognise that God will strike the earth when Jesus will return. They were more concerned with the trees and animals who were missing, clearing up the waste, rather than going forward to preach and teach the gospel (see Matthew ch.28 v18-20). They had a pointless mission.

It was a prophecy against Gog. This was the last time the prophet Ezekiel prophesied against the nations. Looking at Gog (see Ezekiel ch.38 - ch.39), you can see the picture forming:

Vast amounts of plunder.

Rich with livestock.

Even more possessions.

The world revolves around them.

It is a pity that it will all come to nothing, like the Fall of Babylon. All the possession will be gone (see Revelation ch.18).

- - - - - - - -

When a strong man, fully armed, guards his own house, his possessions are safe. Luke ch.11 v21

Jesus was driving out a demon that was mute, but the person couldn't even speak. When the man who had been mute spoke again, some of the Pharisees said. 'By Beelzebub, the prince of demons, he is driving out demons'. Jesus knew what they were thinking, he said to them, 'If Satan is divided against himself, how can his kingdom stand?' (see Luke ch.11 v18).

What it means that Satan gives the demon power but his entire kingdom would destroy itself eventually. Likewise, Satan is a strong man but if someone comes to take his demons away, the same man would be stronger than Satan. Jesus was pointing out that he was more powerful than Satan and then Satan's possessions would be gone away when the judgement starts.

- - - - - - - -

Selling their possessions and goods, they gave to anyone as he had need. Acts ch.2 v45

In the early church with the fellowship of the believers. They devoted themselves to: The apostle's teaching. The fellowship with one another. The breaking the bread and the prayers of the believers.

All the believers were together and had everything in common. Selling their possessions, they gave to the poor. Now a man named Ananias sold a piece of land and gave it to the apostles, but he kept back part of it for himself (see Acts ch.5 v1-2). Then the apostle Peter said, 'Ananias how is it that Satan had filled your heart and you have lied to the church'. Ananias fell down dead and great fear seized all who heard what had happened (Acts ch.5 v5).

The possessions were to be given to the poor, not to some rich people who think that they might extend the gospel to others. It is the poor who need the money and possessions. They gave of themselves the goods and the fields to help the poor, they shared everything they had.

- - - - - - - -

For the world offers only a craving for physical pleasure, a craving for everything we see, and pride in our achievements and possessions. These are not from the Father, but are from this world.   1 John ch.2 v16 (NLT)

The apostle John's letters were written in about AD 93. He was a first cousin of Jesus, his mother was Salome, a sister of Mary (see Matthew ch.27 v56). He was a fisherman going out to fish in the Sea of Galilee (see Mark ch.1 v19-20). The believers are not of this world which is controlled by Satan and organised against God. With fearsome things that many of the people on this earth might have against you and your faith. This is not a happy place for any believers (see Hebrews ch.11 v33-38).

The earth offers a craving for possessions which means that we are not to pursue it, it is of this world. It is a pride for our achievements. Jesus was not interested in having possessions, he was going to save souls by his death of the cross. He didn't have any money or a home to go to.

$\mathcal{P}$roperty

Property is a piece of land owned, an asset or something which will bring profit or income.

Now the Israelites settled in Egypt in the region of Goshen. They acquired property there and were fruitful and increased greatly in number. Genesis ch.47 v27

When Jacob entered Egypt to find out where his son Joseph was, he thought he had lost him with Joseph's brother's giving him the coat which was bloodied. Joseph had sent carts to take Jacob and his family, to collect Jacob's children and their wives (see Genesis ch.45 v19-20).

They were indeed shepherds but the Egyptians didn't trust their flocks and herds. They trampled over the River Nile where all of the good land will be and likely ruin the crops. So they settled in Goshen, away from the land of Egypt. Close to the land of Palestine on the Mediterranean Sea (see Genesis ch.46 v31-34). They acquired property there and greatly increased in numbers because the land was good for sheep. Rich grass around a lake just before entering the Mediterranean Sea.

- - - - - - - -

In all cases of illegal possession of an ox, a donkey, a sheep, a garment, or any other lost property about which someone says, "This is mine," both parties are to bring the cases before the judges. The one whom the judges declare guilty must pay back double to his neighbour. Exodus ch.22 v9

The Israelites were driven out of Egypt because of God sending the plagues. It was a very long time. For 430 years becoming slaves under the Pharaoh (see Exodus 12 v40). A new Pharaoh who didn't understand what Joseph had done, he collected all the grain and distributed it for seven years whilst the famine was there in Egypt.

They entered the Mount of Sinai and God met them there. He gave his instructions to Moses and he appointed judges over the people (see Deuteronomy ch.16 v18). If two people had any stolen property they would go before the judges who decided who was telling the truth. Things purchased like property, a sheep or garment.

- - - - - - - -

"When you make an agreement with your neighbour to buy or sell property, you must not take advantage of each other. Leviticus ch.25 v14 (NLT)

The correct way for the Israelites to live together. They didn't take advantage over the poor. Each one had his own property and regardless when the time came for the Year of Jubilee to proclaim liberty over the land. You are to sell and buy from your countryman on the basis of the number of years since the Jubilee (see Leviticus ch.25 v8-55). Do it properly and don't take advantage over the impoverished of any destitute people.

- - - - - - - -

And the land on the east side of the Jordan will be your property from the Lord. But if you fail to keep your word, then you will have sinned against the Lord, and you may be sure that your sin will find you out. Numbers ch.32 v22-23 (NLT)

When the Israelites went in to the Promised Land, the Reubenites and Gadites who had very large herds of flocks saw that the land of Jazer and Gilead were suitable for livestock (see Numbers ch.32 v1). They came to Moses and Eleazar the priest and said, 'Can we have this property for ourselves'. It was outside of the Promised Land before the Jordan River, it was a place where Ammon was, past the border of Moab. The land of the Philistines was close to the Mediterranean Sea on the coastal plains whereas most of the rest of the land was hill-country.

Moses asked God to decide. The leaders of Reuben and Gad sought to ensure Moses that they did not wish to shirk their duty in helping to conquer the land. They would join their brothers in battle but wished to leave their families and livestock behind in the territory outside. God said, 'The Reuben and Gad must cross the land and conquer it before they can return to their homes'.

- - - - - - - -

The prince must not take any of the inheritance of the people, driving them off their property. He is to give his sons their inheritance out of his own property, so that none of my people will be separated from his property. Ezekiel ch.46 v18

Many years later, when Ezekiel the priest who had been taken away to Babylon as an exile. He still had an image of what the temple looked like. The temple at Jerusalem had been broken down by the Babylonian Empire, so there was nothing left in Judah, it all was ruined and burned down.

The prince in the new temple (see Ezekiel ch.40 - ch.48) would leave the people of Israel alone and not take their property away from them. It was the same law as Moses wrote down, based on the words of God on Mount Sinai (see Numbers ch.34 and 1 Kings ch.21 v1-3).

- - - - - - - -

Everyone who has given up houses or brothers or sisters or father or mother or children or property, for my sake, will receive a hundred times as much in return and will inherit eternal life. Matthew ch.19 v29 (NLT)

In the New Testament, Jesus explains why he did not go after the rich young man, he left him to go away. Riches or property have hampered the young man who wanted to enter eternal life. Jesus reason is that we have to give up property to serve him. If you do so, you can receive 100 times as much.

Those who live according to the sinful nature have their minds set on what that nature desires .. the mind of sinful man is death. Romans ch.8 v5-6

Jesus taught as a believer we must not think of property which comes from Satan, but think of working for the Lord. To save the souls of men who are satisfied with what the property gives them. The work of property is time-consuming and takes up a much of the duration we have left on this earth.

Jesus said, "It is hard for a rich man to enter the kingdom of heaven." Matthew ch.19 v23

The apostle Peter answered him, 'We have left everything to follow you'. Jesus said to him, 'When the Son of Man sits on his throne, you will have followed me and you will be rewarded' (see Matthew ch.19 v28). Property is on this earth only; nothing will follow you when you are dead. The fact is when the earth is finally over Jesus Christ will sit on his throne. Then you will be free to enter the kingdom of heaven with what God has decided to give you.

Prosperity

Prosperity is to flourish, to get on, to turn out well.

The next seven years will be a period of great prosperity throughout the land of Egypt. But afterward there will be seven years of famine so great that all the prosperity will be forgotten in Egypt. Genesis ch.41 v29-30 (NLT)

The dream of Pharaoh where he saw cows coming up out of the river and he saw ears of corn on a single stalk. The first ones were plentiful but the last seven were ugly and thin. Nobody could explain what that meant, even the magicians and wise men of Egypt (see Genesis ch.41 v8). The chief cupbearer remembered Joseph, he could answer Pharaoh's dreams. Joseph an outcast said, 'It was the same dream. Pharaoh with the seven best crops in the land to seven years of famine'. Pharaoh took him from prison and became the second highest rank in the land of Egypt (see Genesis ch.41 v41). From the darkest prison to the whole land of Egypt, it was remarkable!

Prosperity indicates how the produce of the land can also affect people.

- - - - - - - - -

See, I set before you life and prosperity, death and destruction. Deuteronomy ch.30 v15

Moses at the end of his life, before they embarked to go into the Promised Land. He set before the people and he saw life with God's instruction, death without even thinking about God.

God said they will forsake me and break the covenant I made with them. On that day I will become angry with them and forsake them; I will hide my face from them, and they will be destroyed. Deuteronomy ch.31 v16-17

God knew that Israel would be defeated and cast away. Israel didn't come back from the exile, while a remnant of Judah returned. It made a sorrowful picture of what happened in the book of Kings and Chronicles.

For I (Moses) know that after my death you are sure to become utterly corrupt and to turn from the way I have commanded you. In days to come, disaster will fall upon you because you will do evil in the sight of the Lord and provoke him to anger by what your hands have made. Deuteronomy ch.31 v29

This is what will happen as the people acted out of their chosen idols. Prosperity only gives well-being if God controls the land. It was a choice that prosperity brings; but the Israelites failed to do as God expected.

- - - - - - - -

You will watch with envy as I pour out prosperity on the people of Israel. But no members of your family will ever live out their days. 1 Samuel ch.2 v32 (NLT)

In the days of Eli, the priest the practice in the temple of the Lord was dreadful and appalling. He couldn't, or wouldn't manage his sons in what they were doing. A man of God went to Eli and spoke the very words of the Lord (see 1 Samuel ch.2 v27-34). Eli didn't respond to his message and his family were ruined, both of his sons were dead on the same day as the Philistines fought against Israel. They took the ark of the covenant away to their land of the Philistines (see 1 Samuel ch.4 v17).

God maintained the boy Samuel to be his priest instead of Eli. Prosperity will return to Israel, but it will take a very long while to give David the throne of Israel.

- - - - - - - -

Good planning and hard work lead to prosperity, but hasty shortcuts lead to poverty. Proverbs ch.21 v5 (NLT)

Prosperity doesn't come unless you work hard, avoiding short-cuts which lead eventually to ruin. If you had sheep working in the field and didn't bother about it:

No shepherd to take care of it.

No pen to keep it in at night.

No wolves or bears could attack it.

No worries if it got sick.

No concerns if it got lonely.

No thought that if the grass will die away.

No distress that the sheep would get out.

No bother about the sex of the animal.

The sheep will die, then what would you do? Short-cuts lead to poverty and you will have to do more effort. Like good planning and hard work. Each worry has to be considered if you want prosperity.

- - - - - - - -

Don't ever promote the peace and prosperity of those nations. If you follow these instructions, you will be strong and will enjoy the good things the land produces, and you will leave this prosperity to your children forever. Ezra ch.9 v12 (NLT)

After the exile, Judah responded and went back to the Promised Land. The whole company numbered 42,360 and they had many animals (see Ezra ch.2 v64-67). God said to the people, 'If you follow these instructions, you will be strong and overcome the people living in the land, rebuilding the temple of the Lord.'

Prosperity will continue to follow the children provided they obey the words of God. It is only a small amount of people there under 43,000 but if they consistently obey the words of God, they can start building a new temple and the walls around the city of David and begin again. God doesn't need a lot of people: he can do it gradually if the people listen to what he is saying.

- - - - - - - -

Everyone will live in peace and prosperity, enjoying their own grapevines and fig trees, for there will be nothing to fear. Micah ch.4 v4 (NLT)

In the Old Testament peace and prosperity will go together. If peace is what you want, then prosperity will eventually come along. If prosperity is a key, then peace is part of that. Enjoy your grapes and figs!

Take a fig tree is a general rule that is it relies on the soil around it. If the fig tree is not old enough then it will not bear fruit. It is from the mulberry family and is a very important food in Israel. Whereas the sycamore fig tree can be easily distinguished by its mottled bark which flakes off in great irregular masses. So you have to find which tree it is. A vine is a cultivated shrub or tree that is widely cultivated in Israel. It became a symbol of the people. The grapes were used for pressing which was often done with the feet, the juice was left in pots of goatskins. The wine needs work done to enjoy the fruit of the grapes.

Both trees need work done to prepare the land for cultivation. It relies on being prepared and doing the correct procedure. It is not coming out of the house, enjoying in the garden and eating grapes and figs in the sun. Prosperity has to do with hard work.

$\mathcal{P}rovision$

Provision is something that is contributed, prepared or served.

This bread of ours we took was hot for our provision from our houses on the day we departed to come to you. But now look, it is dry and mouldy. And these wineskins which we filled were new, and see, they are torn; and these our garments and our sandals have become old because of the very long journey. Joshua ch.9 v12-13 (NKJV)

The Gibeonite deception. When the people of Gibeon heard what had been done to Jericho and Ai, they sent a delegation to Joshua to make a treaty with them. They said we have come a long way (see Joshua ch.9 v9). The men of Israel did not enquire of the Lord and they made a treaty with them, a sworn oath to them by the Lord, the God of Israel. Three days after their treaty with them the people found out that they were neighbours (see Joshua ch.9 v16).

Bad food, poor water and worn-out clothing but not asking for the Lord's help means the provision is not what it seems.

- - - - - - - -

Moreover, He called for a famine in the land; He destroyed all the provision of bread. Psalm ch.105 v16 (NKJV)

This Psalm is an exhortation for Israel to worship and trust in the Lord. It deals with the problems that God encountered when the time of the Israelites who shared the Lord's wonderful acts. It emphasises, Joseph who was a slave but God sent a man ahead to rescue Egypt from the famine and the people under Jacob were saved. Only one man was chosen, but he was shackled on his feet and his neck was put in irons. He was imprisoned unjustly (see Psalm ch.105 v17-18).

This famine destroyed all the provision of grain both in Palestine, all the provisions were gone.

- - - - - - - -

Solomon also had twelve district governors over all Israel, who supplied provisions for the king and the royal household. 1 Kings ch.4 v7

Solomon was king over Israel. Following king David, he created building projects from his land. They entered the most advanced culture of the period including God's temple and the royal palace (see Ecclesiastes ch.2 v4-6). Small wonder that king Solomon had district governors who supplied food for the royal household. The governors had all his provisions and they served the king for only one month in that year.

- - - - - - - -

And the king appointed for them a daily provision of the king's delicacies and of the wine which he drank, and three years of training for them, so that at the end of that time they might serve before the king. Daniel ch.1 v5 (NKJV)

King Jehoiachin of Judah was ready to revolt against Babylon. He thought that Egypt would come to his aid (see 2 Kings ch.24 v7). Not really, the main Babylonian army captured Jerusalem and exiling the king and the most important people (see 2 Kings ch.24 v10-14). Daniel was among them (see Daniel ch.1 v3-5). King Nebuchadnezzar, he ordered that Ashpenaz, chief of his court officials to care for them so that they might aid his service.

Daniel didn't want the rich food, he wanted vegetables to eat and water to drink (see Daniel ch.1 v12). The Israelites considered food from king Nebuchadnezzar's table to be contaminated because the first portion of it was offered to idols. Likewise, a potion of the wine was poured out on a pagan altar. Ceremonially unclean animals were used and were neither slaughtered nor prepared according to the regulations of the law of God. Vegetables and water were much better for the provision of food.

- - - - - - - -

Supplement your faith with a generous provision of moral excellence, and moral excellence with knowledge, and knowledge with self-control, and self-control with patient endurance, and patient endurance with godliness, and godliness with brotherly affection, and brotherly affection with love for everyone. 2 Peter ch.1 v5-8 (NLT)

In the New Testament the provision of moral excellence was preferred.

These virtues that will produce a well-documented fruitful life: for excellence, knowledge, self-control, endurance, godliness, affection and love. This is what we should be aiming for; love for one another. This is a provision for a believer. But we don't start with love, there are several more points to encounter, starting with excellence and knowledge.

$\mathscr{R}$esources

Resource is a means of a support. Like occupying or storing anything.

It doesn't appear in the Old Testament, why not? Because God holds his Israelites in his hand and gives them what they need through the Promised Land. Whether they do good or bad things. The resources are God himself. Whereas in the New Testament the reasons are different and as you can see:

Joanna, the wife of Chuza, Herod's business manager; Susanna; and many others who were contributing their own resources to support Jesus and his disciples. Luke ch.8 v3 (NLT)

Jesus travelled around from one town and village to another preaching the good news of the kingdom of God (see Luke ch.3 v3). He left his home and went with his disciples, he didn't have any money, he didn't have any food his clothing was made up by his friends (see John ch.19 v23-24). He didn't even have a staff to support himself neither did he have a coat nor a bag to keep things in (see Matthew ch.10 v10).

When Jesus was crucified out of the city of Jerusalem the women who had followed him from Galilee were watching. They stood at a distance, contemplating these things (see Luke ch.23 v49). He was dependent upon the women who cared for him and kept him safe. The resources they provided to support Jesus and his disciples.

- - - - - - - -

Here's the lesson: Use your worldly resources to benefit others and make friends. Then, when your earthly possessions are gone, they will welcome you to an eternal home. Luke ch.16 v9 (NLT)

The parable of the Shrewd Manager. There was a rich man whose manager was accused of wasting his possessions. The manager lost his job so he decided to call in each of his rich man debtors, reducing the amount they owed to the master to a reasonable figure. He might go to one of them to be a friend, to save him from his dishonesty in dealing with the rich man.

Jesus said, 'For the people of this world are more shrewd in dealing with their own kind than are the righteous people.' What about the thoughts about true riches when you die? Resources need to be the type that would welcome you to the eternal home, not the dishonest way of living on the earth (see Luke ch.16 v13).

You are of your father the devil, and the desires of your father you want to do. He was a murderer from the beginning, and does not stand in the truth, because there is no truth in him. When he speaks a lie, he speaks from his own resources, for he is a liar and the father of it. John ch.8 v44 (NKJV)

Jesus said to them, 'If God was your Father, would you love me?' (see John ch.8 v42). He told the message to the Jews, the people who thought they would be called God's friends. Jesus told them that their relationship was indeed Satan, the prince of devils. It points to a definition of will, their problem was basically spiritual. Being orientated towards Satan they were bent on murder (see John ch.8 v37) and they would eventually succeed. Satan would have the resources necessary to kill the 'Righteous One' (see Acts ch.7 v52).

Jesus was only sacrificing for all of us (see Isaiah ch.53). He was doing the will of his Father and Satan will have to admit defeat. Eventually Jesus would overcome Satan (see Revelation ch.19 v11-21, ch.20 v10). The resources of the good rather than the bad.

For God is the one who provides seed for the farmer and then bread to eat. In the same way, he will provide and increase your resources and then produce a great harvest of generosity in you. 2 Corinthians ch.9 v10 (NLT)

The apostle Paul remarks under Sowing Generously, 'Whoever sows sparingly will also reap sparingly'. For God loves a cheerful giver (2 Corinthians ch.9 v6-7). We eat several times a day where God has provided food for us. Not local food from our fields, but other foods where the hot regions and fresh water prepare for us to live. We have an abundant source of food, like in the supermarket. Why do you not give back to God what he has so kindly given you?

The effect of generous giving on the part of the Corinthian churches will extend beyond Jerusalem. The destination of their gift to the church as a whole causing prayer and praise to God. This is what really matters. The resources of us each giving, will extend to be able to function as a church and give resources to the poor, not locked-up and saved in a bank.

- - - - - - - -

I pray that from his glorious, unlimited resources he will empower you with inner strength through his Spirit. Ephesians ch.3 v16 (NLT)

The empowering to fortify the believer's inner life, especially under trial. For the indwelling strength that the Holy Spirit will come within our lives. This makes us mighty and powerful to work for Jesus. Carrying on his message to the weak people, to go out and spread the word preaching and teaching for his glory (see Matthew ch.28 v18-20). To equip the church whilst here on earth. This is what the apostle Paul meant for his 'unlimited resources' so that Christ may dwell in your hearts through faith.

Rewards

Rewards are given in return for good work or in recognition of merit for the performance of any act of service.

Boaz said, "May you be richly rewarded by the Lord, the God of Israel, under whose wings you have come to take refuge." Ruth ch.2 v12

Naomi and Ruth came home to Israel, because there was a great famine in the land of Israel so they departed and left. Ruth was a Moabitess so Noami told her to go back to her people but she didn't (see Ruth ch.1 v8). She was determined to go with Naomi to her home in Israel. She said to Naomi, 'Your people will be my people and your God will be my God' (see Ruth ch.1 v16).

Eventually Ruth married Boaz (see Ruth ch.4 v13) and she became pregnant. Her son was the grandfather of king David (see Ruth ch.4 v21-22). The Lord rewarded her for her devotion to Naomi, she became the grandmother for the ruler of Israel. But she was a Moabitess, an alien and an outsider.

- - - - - - - -

Wise words bring many benefits, and hard work brings rewards. Proverbs ch.12 v14 (NLT)

Wise words will give comfort to the heartless. It contrasts Jesus' teaching and Jewish legalistic discourses. The crowds were amazed at Jesus tuition because they understood what he was talking about (see Matthew ch.7 v28-29). Hard work brings rewards. Jesus teaching involved considerable effort to heal the sick, to silence the crowds, to give of himself and his expert guidance. Nothing like that has been taught, ever again. You forget what Jesus did in three years, he emphasised the power of God through his ministry. He did what no man has every done.

- - - - - - - -

Your princes are rebellious, and companions of thieves; everyone loves bribes, and follows after rewards. They do not defend the fatherless, nor does the cause of the widow come before them. Isaiah ch.1 v23 (NKJV)

It was a rebellious nation that the prophet Isaiah saw concerning Judah and Jerusalem, during the reigns of Uzziah through to Hezekiah (see Isaiah ch.1 v1). Most of the kings were good but Ahaz was evil. After king Hezekiah died his boy was the worst king that ever lived, he was king Manasseh who spent fifty-five years on the throne (see 2 Kings ch.21 v1-18). But the prophet Isaiah didn't see him, he died before he came along.

Isaiah saw that they victimised the widow and the fatherless; the poor females that should have been protected by the state. The thieves and everyone who lives in that region. It starts with the top, the princes who should have know better than anyone. The rule is for the king to outline his policy and the rest of the country follows (see 1 Samuel ch.8 v10-18). They do not think of the rewards that God will present to them when they have died. 'The books were opened' which means that every person will come to God to be judged. For the writing was there and all will see (Psalm ch.62 v12; Revelation ch.20 v12).

- - - - - - - -

I the Lord search the heart and examine the mind, to reward a man according to his conduct, according to what his deeds deserve. Jeremiah ch.17 v10

It is God who reflected the earth and everybody in it. Whether it is in the past, now present in the current days, or in the future. God writes down in his books everything you do. Evil and bad things or the good and kind events that you do. They are present at the judgement when you will face God.

What is he going to say to you? What rewards will he give to you?

- - - - - - - -

But if you tell me the dream and explain it, you will receive from me gifts and rewards and great honour. So tell me the dream and interpret it for me. Daniel ch.2 v6

While king Nebuchadnezzar slept, he had a dream and his mind was deeply troubled. He couldn't remember his dream when he was finally awake, parts of it will come and go, but he could not sleep at all worrying about it. Dreams were really important and the king had his misfortune not to bring it to mind. So the king asked the magicians, enchanters, sorcerers and astrologers to tell him about his dream. It's a lot of people with all different skills but they could not remember his dream. Nobody can. So the king exploded with rage, he said:

"If you do not tell me what my dream meant.

If you do not interpret it for me.

I will have you cut into pieces.

Your house will be turned into piles of rubble."

Daniel went away and asked God to tell him what the dream meant. The gifts of the king were not part of what Daniel had in mind. He was saving his people his exiles from Jerusalem. He didn't want to be killed.

You must keep your gifts for yourself and give your rewards to someone else. Nevertheless, I will read the writing for the king and tell him what it means. Daniel ch.5 v17

After king Nebuchadnezzar had died, a new king was on his throne and he was the grandson, king Belshazzar. He was having an orgy of merrymaking and blasphemy, he was drinking wine when a hand appeared writing on the plaster of the wall, near the lampstand. The king watched the hand writing and his face turned pale and his knees knocked together and his legs gave way. He was terrified and stunned. But he knew that that the Lord had written for the king personally (see Daniel ch.5 v5-6). The same cause as when king Nebuchadnezzar had a dream. The magicians, enchanters, astrologers and diviners they could not read the writing of the hand that wrote on the plaster of the wall. Why? Because the writing was not difficult to explain in the Aramaic words, but in their significance. There was no context that could make these words seems relevant to the king or his wise men. It reads: *mn' mn' tql prs*.

Daniel knew that the king was doomed and he said, 'Keep your rewards to someone else'. The king had sinned and not due to ignorance. He defiled God by using the gold vessels taken from the house of the Lord and he praised idols and did not honour God. He forgot the words of God, but gave rewards to those who could tell him what they meant. This very night the king was slain and the Medes took over the kingdom (see Daniel ch.5 v30).

- - - - - - - -

Rejoice and be glad, because great is your reward in heaven, for in the same way they persecuted the prophets who were before you. Matthew ch.5 v12

Jesus said, 'Great is your reward in heaven'. Why did he say that? The Israelites persecuted the prophets. Not one, but several over the years. They left them to die (see Jeremiah ch.38 v6-9). The prophets suffered, abused and ill treated in the early days and now it is the same as we are going through. If you think that your sufferings from the devil are cruel and malicious, be thankful that you are protected by the Holy Spirit and will win when it is over. Regardless of the evil plots by all of the evil spirits but the rewards are in a future place, in heaven.

When tempted, no-one should say, "God is tempting me." For God cannot be tempted by evil, nor does he tempt anyone; but each one is tempted when, by his own evil desire, he is dragged away and enticed. James ch.1 v13-14

Don't think that suffering is solely due to God. For Satan and his fallen angels can make life hard and difficult to pass through. It is you who are tempted by your own evil life. It is easy for Satan and the fallen angels to encourage you to sin because of your past misdeeds.

God doesn't tempt you to do wrong, but the rewards he offers to you to break to power of the Satan and he will leave you with his precious word (see Matthew ch.4 v1-11).

- - - - - - - - -

For God does not show favouritism. Romans ch.2 v11

He acts as a counsel, to warn those who with personal problems: He searches the heart. He examines the mind. He acts as a barrister or advocate. Who can think that they may have decided to act in the dark, or do things in the daytime where no-one sees? He searches and examines all people, whether ever they go and writes it in his books (see Psalm ch.139). God in his judging will be completely fair and seriously true.

He watches everyone closely, examining every person on earth. The Lord examines both the righteous and the wicked. Psalm ch.11 v4-5 (NLT)

The Scriptures explain from the Old Testament to the New Testament. The works you have done on the earth will be judged accordingly, whether right or wrong and there will be no favouritism or appeasement from God. When we die, nothing can be taken from this earth, there is no thought that we can buy God off from the writing in his books.

The rewards will be there when Jesus Christ comes again.

- - - - - - - -

Without faith it is impossible to please God, because anyone who comes to him must believe that he exists and that he rewards those who earnestly seek him. Hebrews ch.11 v6

If you don't have faith that saves you and believe God doesn't exist, there is no help for you. The Bible says that it is a fool who doesn't believe in God (see Psalm ch.14 v1). It goes on to say:

The people are corrupt in what they do.

The people deeds are vile and appalling.

The people just fail to do anything good.

It's a lesson worth noting. Nothing good can come out of them if they are evil and corrupt. It is a sign that we respect God and his commandments. The rules are plain: without God, everyone does what is good for them and regardless of the people around them. Violence, malice, hostility and hatred all come from Satan, who likes to have people thinking bad thoughts.

There is no one who does good, not even one. Psalm ch.14 v3

He rewards those who come to him and earnestly seek him with faith and trust. The only way is to follow Jesus Christ. To come to him as Saviour and Lord.

Saviour: coming to Jesus in repentance for the wrong things we have done.

Lord: depending on Jesus for what we should do in this life.

- - - - - - - -

Jesus said, "Behold, I am coming soon! My reward is with me, and I will give to everyone according to what he has done." Revelation ch.22 v12

Jesus will certainly return. He left us alone for over two centuries with the Holy Spirit helping those who come to him. He waits, and still waits for the last person who comes to him with faith to believe. Only the heavenly Father knows when it is time to return (see Matthew ch.24 v36). Then when he returns, it will be very different. The believers will be transported into the air (see 1 Thessalonians ch.4 v16-17). The plagues will start forming and Satan knows his end has come. God will wipe the earth clean again, change it back to what God has intended (see 2 Peter ch.3 v7; Isaiah ch.65 v17).

Jesus said, 'My reward is with me I will give it to those on the earth who have acted out of love' (see 1 Peter ch.4 v7-8). If you believe in God, he loves us and will reward any person with kindness according to what he has done on the earth.

Riches

Riches are a fortune in having any good thing abundantly supplied or stocked.

Moreover, I will give you what you have not asked for - both riches and honour - so that in your lifetime you will have no equal among kings. 1 Kings ch.3 v13

King Solomon asked God in a dream to give him a discerning heart. This is all he asked for: not long life, riches, power and removing his enemies from him. God was pleased that Solomon had asked for this but he promised to give him the power of wisdom and riches. The two goes together: if the wisdom is not there the riches will be used up very quickly. The riches go with hard work and wisdom is the key to doing this for your life on earth. Riches will make king Solomon mightier than all the other kings (1 Kings ch.4 v29-34).

- - - - - - - -

Look at these wicked people—enjoying a life of ease while their riches multiply. Psalm ch.73 v12 (NLT)

Many people have riches passed on by their ancestors. Or building a company out of nothing, even figures of sport and fame. No-one can say only the riches were for the good, but the wicked as well earned a place of riches that multiply. They take a life of ease while we all have to work for a long time to earn some money. You have income and expenditure, try as we can we can earn a little more each year. Many people don't have the luxury to go on working until they die and pass from this life on earth.

- - - - - - - -

Riches won't help on the day of judgement, but right living can save you from death. Proverbs ch.11 v4 (NLT)

We only have a short time on this earth, only a few years. Then what will happen? As we die the riches stay on this planet, we don't take anything away with us. Even the powerful Egyptians left treasures behind over the years.

They have embedded it in the pyramids but later they will be robbed away and will take nothing with them.

'Right Living' can save you from death. It is not people who are poor meaning they couldn't get a job. Poor means a lot more than that.

The poor can be made up of several conditions:

Famine is always there as crops fail and the ground is hard.

Squalid conditions they can't look after their homes.

People on the streets without any home to go to.

Aliens running away from dangerous conditions.

Believers and others kept in prison for doing good works.

Widows and the fatherless who looked after children.

- - - - - - - -

There is another serious problem I have seen under the sun. Hoarding riches harms the saver. Money is put into risky investments that turn sour, and everything is lost. In the end, there is nothing left to pass on to one's children. We all come to the end of our lives as naked and empty-handed as on the day we were born. We can't take our riches with us. Ecclesiastes ch.5 v13-15 (NLT)

Hoarding riches harms the saver. Why? They think that turning money into wealth gives a lot of protection, keeps you away from danger, people have a large house with possessions, turning money into the retirement. But it is all lost, what about accidents or illness for your body?

I remember a person who worked hard. He saved up a lot of money and he was going to spend it with his wife. He had a caravan and was going around the earth, he was counting the days when he would be free to retire. Only a few days before his retirement his wife passed away. All that his money was wasted, he could have spent it over the years, but he didn't. He saved it up.

Don't think that gold or silver is the answer to your problems. What about your riches when you die?

- - - - - - - -

Yes, your wisdom has made you very rich, and your riches have made you very proud. Ezekiel ch.28 v5 (NLT)

There is a danger that you might be proud of your riches. God hates the proud and will do everything to humble them. They are sinful and ruthless, they take away from the widows and the poor. They will be thoughtless, inattentive and desperate to make money. The riches make you hard, like 'Scrooge' in Charles Dicken's book, 'A Christmas Carol'.

The Lord detests the proud; they will surely be punished ... Haughty eyes, a proud heart, and evil actions are all sin. Proverbs ch.16 v5, ch.21 v4 (NLT)

A proud heart is sin. It is a very wise individual who can provide wealth and riches and be prevented from from sinning. This is the Holy Spirit's work and will lead you to make actions that are right and proper. It is not riches that are sinful, it is the type of person that you might end up creating.

- - - - - - - -

Stands for those who hear, but as they go on their way they are choked by life's worries, riches and pleasures, and they do not mature. Luke ch.8 v14

Jesus taught the parable of The Sower. He said that, 'Some seed fell among the thorns, but the thorns stifled the word of God'. They heard, but did not respond in kind:

Worries they have too much to lose anyway.

Riches they don't want to give anything away.

Pleasures they want you to restrict your activities.

Friends who have cars, aeroplanes, ships and mansions.

They don't mature, they stay where they are put, they have an inability to go out preaching or teaching the word of God. You can see them going to church, sitting in the pews or chairs. They are doing nothing and they don't respond to what God wants. He doesn't want you sitting in the church every week. He wants you to go out spreading the news for all the lost (see Matthew ch.28 v19-20).

- - - - - - - -

The depth of the riches of the wisdom and knowledge of God! How unsearchable his judgements, and his path beyond tracing out! Romans ch.11 v33

Our life is dead to sin but Jesus makes us alive through the Holy Spirit. We deserve to be punished by God's wrath against mankind. When Jesus died on the cross, he rescued us, made us more than conquerors. He selected and chose us for his kingdom. How much we owe to God for the riches of his wisdom and knowledge. He sent his son Jesus to save us. Out of the whole world and all it's people, past and current and in the future. You are special to God for all the hundreds and thousands of people for all nations.

You are selected only by God, just you.

- - - - - - - -

This is God's plan: Both Gentiles and Jews who believe the Good News share equally in the riches inherited by God's children. Ephesians ch.3 v6 (NLT)

This is God's plan, we are saved by Jesus' sacrificial death on the cross, we have been made alive through the Holy Spirit who came to us and makes his home in our lives. We have believed in Jesus and equally share in the bountiful riches by inheriting God's heirs. We are saved from now on, we are going to heaven and will sit with him in glory, in his greatness, honour and recognition.

What happens now is that we discard riches and work towards Jesus coming again. We only have a short time on this earth. We currently ignore riches in this world, we look towards his righteousness and certainly will enter his kingdom of heaven. The riches belong to Satan (see Luke ch.4 v5-7).

They went around in sheepskins and goatskins, destitute, persecuted and ill-treated - the world was not worthy of them. They wandered in deserts and mountains, and in caves and holes in the ground. Hebrews ch.11 v37-38

This is what the disciple is going through. No riches or wealth or assets. The riches hide you from God and you surround yourself in a big house where the gardens protect you for what is happening around. You wander around going from room to room thinking that you have done well and you should be pleased.

The Lord looks on the poor and he comforts the destitute, but the riches hide yourself away from that. He wants you to go out and look for the poor and tell them the message of his kingdom. How can you do that with clothes fit for a king, beautifully manicured skin, where do you park your flash car?

It doesn't make sense, riches protect you from what you should be doing.

Seeds

The seed grows and it takes on a form like a field of grass which will grow and develop over time.

Then God said, "Let the land sprout with vegetation—every sort of seed-bearing plant, and trees that grow seed-bearing fruit. These seeds will then produce the kinds of plants and trees from which they came." Genesis ch.1 v11 (NLT)

When the seeds fall into the ground, God will water them and the seeds develop into plants and grow. We can't even today make seeds with all our expertise and machines. Hopefully in the weeks to come the seeds will develop in time. It takes a long while for the seed to sprout and turn into whatever plants you decide to grow. This is why God made the plants before he made animals to eat them.

- - - - - - - -

I said, 'Plant the good seeds of righteousness, and you will harvest a crop of love. Plow up the hard ground of your hearts, for now is the time to seek the Lord, that he may come and shower righteousness upon you.' Hosea ch.10 v12 (NLT)

The prophet Hosea lived in the tragic final days of the northern kingdom. During which many kings were murdered by their successors whilst they served the Israelites. Shortly afterwards Israel was captured by the Assyrian Empire, then after BC 722-721 the people in Samaria were taken away bringing the northern kingdom of Israel to an end.

Hosea said, 'Plant the good seeds in your heart'. God will be waiting to see whether the righteousness and love for the Israelites. To sow the seeds of forgiveness and God will respond to you. That certainly didn't happen and Israel was finally exiled away from the Promised Land. Everything comes to a final stop, God sent his prophets and the Israelites ignored them. So what is happening today? Did you understand his prophets? Did you know what the prophets said?

- - - - - - - -

Still other seed fell on good soil, where it produced a crop - a hundred, sixty or thirty times what was sown. He who has ears, let him hear. Matthew ch.13 v8-9

Jesus told the parable of The Sower and we have mentioned it before. He indicated for the good seed on the ground that each will have a different chance of success. The same ground, the water flows by each plant, there is no distinction between the weather, it is all the same type. Why did those plants not grow to the magnitude of the crop? Like a hundred percent.

Because the plants had an excuse to vary the amount of growth that they had produced. Some worked hard for Jesus but some didn't. They were all the same, the seed was the same, but some didn't perform as well as the rest. Some did what Jesus taught, go out and bring in the rest of the people but others sat in the church buildings. They were all believers saved by the work of Jesus his sacrificial work on the cross. They were all saved. But the crop was different. Jesus said, 'He who has ears, let him hear'.

It is a warning and there is a different growth for the seeds in the kingdom of God. Jesus said, 'Remember the things I taught you!' Consider the 'crowns', do you know why he told you that? He is expecting you to produce the fruit of righteousness.

- - - - - - - -

It is like a mustard seed, which is the smallest seed you plant in the ground. Yet when planted; it grows and becomes the largest of all garden plants, with such big branches that the birds of the air can perch in its shade. Mark ch.4 v31-32

Jesus taught the parable of the Mustard Seed. The mustard seed is the smallest seed you can ever buy. It is very tiny and you might mix it with sand otherwise you will have too many seeds in the ground when you sow. The mustard seed when it grows it will be magnificent. It will be the largest plant that you can grow in your garden, even the big branches where the birds can rest in its shade.

Why did he tell it? Because the smallest seed, ignored by most gardeners, they thought it was basically soil. A small seed but God recognised it for what it was. Only a small seed that will not be recognised by the church, going to the back, not singing well, certainly not up at the front directing the message. However, the seed will grow and will reproduce a splendid plant that even the birds will rejoice in it.

This is the fruit of studying the Scriptures (see 2 Timothy ch.3 v16-17). Even the birds that have no place in the garden will arrive and shade in it. It will be impressive and striking but the mustard seed didn't even know that. It is like the seed that grows into a big tree overshadowing the other crops around it, It will be an excellent tree that God would be proud of it. The lonely, poor widow putting in some smallest copper coins in the temple treasury, but Jesus noticed her and she was not even aware of it (see Luke ch.21 v2). This is like the treasure in heaven.

- - - - - - - -

Remember this: Whoever sows sparingly will also reap sparingly, and whoever sows generously will also reap generously. Each man should give what he has decided in his heart to give, not reluctantly or under compulsion, for God loves a cheerful giver. 2 Corinthians ch.9 v6-7

The apostle Paul is talking about giving, but he uses the word for seed. Anybody who sows sparingly will reap sparingly. Which means that an individual has a seed which he wants to pass on, like the gospel of Jesus. If he doesn't go and do it, the effect will be that most people will pass him by. The reaping will be disappointing. But it is important that he sows to anybody, he doesn't know from which the Holy Spirit moves, he sows repeatedly and reaps consistently.

Consider Billy Graham, he expects that when he is preaching many souls will be moved. He trusts that the Lord will make his message clear that several more will believe. Don't be dismayed, many people will not believe but some will. We are expected to sow seeds and reap what the Holy Spirit convicts. If we don't do it, how can people think what they are doing is wrong?

- - - - - - - -

Those who are peacemakers will plant seeds of peace and reap a harvest of righteousness. James ch.3 v18 (NLT)

We are expected to reach those whom we come across, like family, neighbours, work and of course going to the shops. Every time we display what Jesus did, his living, his miracles and his dying, the seeds we show are peaceful to remind us of what Jesus meant to us. It will lead to a harvest of righteousness but we didn't know what the effect the seed will have. This is the only way to get souls from Satan back to God. That means a repentance from sin and a new life in the Holy Spirit.

The seeds we can sow to make the world a better place. It would be better if the believers turned from protesting about anything. To sow the seed of righteousness which will lead the Holy Spirit to convict men and women. Nothing else will matter.

$\mathcal{S}$*tore*

Store as a temporary stock laid up for future use.

Have them gather all the food produced in the good years that are just ahead and bring it to Pharaoh's storehouses. Store it away, and guard it so there will be food in the cities. Genesis ch.41 v35 (NLT)

Joseph told the Pharaoh in his dream to set aside the good years that will come to pass. After that for the seven famine years of famine it will be dreadful and painful. God has told Pharaoh what will happen and it will come to pass, it will be firmly decided (see Genesis ch.41 v32). Store the grain under the authority of Pharaoh to let the Egyptians buy grain for the coming famine. It was so much like the sand of the sea; it was so much that he stopped keeping records (see Genesis ch.41 v49). The Egyptians didn't realise what the years of famine could bring, so they went to Pharaoh for food and they didn't store up the grain for the coming brutal years (see Genesis ch.41 v55, ch.47 v13-26).

The Egyptians didn't believe that the famine would last for a long while but Joseph did. He established it as a law in Egypt that a fifth of the land belongs to Pharaoh, only the land belonging to the priests was spared. Joseph saved all of Egypt and south of Canaan by himself, with God's help and instruction. Nobody in Egypt thought they might need grain, but it was an over-reaction by Joseph, but Pharaoh understood from the dream he was given and he set Joseph up to be his second in command.

- - - - - - - -

At the end of every three years, bring all the tithes of that year's produce and store it in your towns. Deuteronomy ch.14 v28

Later when the Israelites moved out of Egypt, they went to the Mount of Sinai. This is where God gave them further instructions about what he wanted them to do in the Promised Land where they were going.

It was associated with tithing (see Deuteronomy ch.14 v22-29). The people of Israel were to bring gifts to the sons of Aaron, the priests, the Levites who did not have an inheritance in the land but they were serving God. The Israelites stored that year's produce as a tithe to come to God. Tithing was a way of bringing the servants of the Lord (who did not have fields) to carry on with the work of the Lord.

- - - - - - - -

Ants are creatures of little strength, yet they store up their food in the summer. Proverbs ch.30 v25

Even ants, who don't have much vigour and strength found time to store in summer because they had a lot of small ants coming and going. The ants carried the produce little by little and the ants were busily coming to the nest. Yet the Israelites had a lot of strength and God decided to store up the grain each summer for the priests. There is no excuse for the people of the land to forget the tithes that must be made. If ants do it, so can people.

You don't remember the ants, they relied on the summer to store up grain for the winter. Every house had ants in the garden, God is using that to teach us a lesson. The ants are so small and tiny but they are busy finding food. We rely on the shops, but what if they can't supply us with what we need? What do we do? The idea is to store up what is needed and then bring it out when the shops are empty.

- - - - - - - -

He will be the sure foundation for your times, a rich store of salvation and wisdom and knowledge; the fear of the Lord is the key to this treasure. Isaiah ch.33 v6

Isaiah was a great prophet, he wrote of the expansion of the Assyrian Empire with that of the decline of Israel, he warned it will take the Assyrian to overrun Israel. The Babylonian Empire will take over Judah (see Isaiah ch.2 v1). Would the coming of Cyrus the Persian to let them return home? (see Isaiah ch.44 v28). He even talks about the coming of Jesus (see Isaiah ch.7 v14). This is why the prophet Isaiah is known as the great prophet of the Lord.

Store up the good things, like: salvation, wisdom and knowledge. The fear of the Lord is the key to this treasure. He remarked that it is not tithing that the Israelites had to do, but the fear and dread of the Lord. Then the people would see that the priests needed food. When they came back to the Promised Land all of the land was in a dreadful state. The poor people couldn't manage the trees, shrubs and bushes that grew up, the fields had grass and weeds growing in them.

- - - - - - - -

Do not store up for yourselves treasures on earth ... store up for yourselves treasures in heaven ... For where your treasure is, there your heart will be also. Matthew ch.6 v19-21

Jesus reminded his crowds of people not to store up goods like grain and property and money but store up treasures in heaven. It is the same things that the prophet Isaiah wrote, more than seven centuries ago, for concentrating our minds, collecting riches or wisdom and knowledge. Wisdom comes only from God himself. Studying the Bible helps, but wisdom takes time to organise itself, for the Holy Spirit will lead and warn you. Provided you let him guide you and do not concentrate on other things.

Look at the birds of the air; they do not sow or reap or store in barns, and yet your heavenly Father feeds them. Matthew ch.6 v26

Take stock, look around you, think of the birds of the air. Yet they do not store in barns? How could they? Your heavenly Father feeds them and not when you put seed out in the garden. Most birds fly away, but the heavenly Father feeds all of them, even the birds who make their nests in rocky crags (see Job ch.38 v41, ch.39 v29). God looks after the birds when man cannot because they are too far away or the nests are so high in the rocks. God looks after all the birds and animals, he created them and he feeds them. Do you not realise that God provides food? Most animals and birds are still around today.

- - - - - - - -

Sell your possessions and give to those in need. This will store up treasure for you in heaven! Luke ch.12 v33 (NLT)

Store up treasure in heaven: sell your possessions and give to those in need. This is what Jesus wants. He wants us to feed the poor. Look at the poor and feed them with all of your store in barns and other places. It is not taking away what you need, but providing them from your store. He doesn't want us to give more money to the rich, even thought they think they need it. A church collection is a good idea, but it is concentrating on feeding the poor.

Consider this and meditate upon it.

He has scattered abroad his gifts to the poor, his righteousness endures for ever.
2 Corinthians ch.9 v9

God wants you to feed the poor so he scatters his gifts. What does that mean? His reasoning is that the Holy Spirit gives gifts across the world to let the poor be satisfied. If it is only one country, what about the rest of the poor?

Now there three gifts remain; faith hope and love but the greatest of all is love.
1 Corinthians ch.13 v13

So, what do you do with love? Feed the poor, both in this country and other places.

Substance

Substance is something to which qualities or attributes exist, one of those defines wealth or property.

What He (God) did to Dathan and Abiram the sons of Eliab, the son of Reuben: how the earth opened its mouth and swallowed them up, their households, their tents, and all the substance that was in their possession, in the midst of all Israel. Deuteronomy ch.11 v6 (NKJV)

They became insolent before Moses. With them were two hundred and fifty men well-known, community leaders who had been appointed members of the council. They came as a group before Moses and Aaron, and said to them, 'You have gone to far, why do you set yourself above the Lord's community'. Moses said to them, 'Take censors and tomorrow put fire and incense on them before the Lord and he will select those he wants to be holy'.

Korah, Dathan and Abiram and their wives, children and little ones at their tents and the earth swallowed them up, because they had each one had taken a censor at the entrance to the Tent of Meeting. The Lord appeared and the glory of the Lord appeared to the entire assembly (see Numbers ch.16 v1-35). All their substance that was in their possession was gone and the earth swallowed it up. The censor was an important role for the priests that God had insisted, otherwise everybody could do it.

- - - - - - - -

Bless his substance, Lord, and accept the work of his hands; strike the loins of those who rise against him, and of those who hate him, that they rise not again. Deuteronomy ch.33 v11 (NKJV)

Moses blesses the tribes of the Israelites when he came to the tribe of Levi. They didn't have any inheritance in the Promised Land because they were serving the Lord God (see Numbers ch.3 v5-13). They were selected from among the Israelites in place of the first male offspring of every Israelite woman. For all the firstborn are God's when the Lord struck down the plagues in Egypt.

For the tribe of Levi, your relatives, I will compensate them for their service in the Tabernacle. Instead of an allotment of land, I will give them the tithes from the entire land of Israel. Numbers ch.18 v21 (NLT)

Levi's substance was the Lord's, he gave them the tithes of the rest of the Israel. The first produce of their fields and the part of the sacrifice, whatever is set aside from the gifts of the wave offerings for Israelites who were coming to serve God.

- - - - - - - -

Your eyes saw my unformed body. All the days ordained for me were written in your book before one of them came to be. Psalm ch.139 v16

A Psalm of David. He knew that God was watching him wherever he would go, looking after him day and night. He was observing and seeing as he created me in my mother's arms. David was the last one to be visited when Samuel went to Jesse's house (see 1 Samuel ch.16 v11), he was tending the sheep and not party to what Samuel had in mind. Samuel chooses the next king over Israel in front of his brothers and parents. But God knew and was writing in his book for the whole of David's life. His eyes saw David's substance and possessions, yet David could not understand how God had selected him, chose him to be king over Israel and Judah.

A poor boy, last in his father's house. God saw how he reacted and wrote in his book before David knew about it. The book that will last until the judgement. God knew David's heart and that made a real difference. When we fail and go astray, God knew about it, he cared for us and lovingly brought us back to him, he understood and treasured us for himself. Yet that is a wonderful truth about God.

- - - - - - - -

Yet when he is found, he must restore sevenfold; he may have to give up all the substance of his house. Proverbs ch.6 v31 (NKJV)

It requires him to pay in full (see Exodus ch.22 v1-9), it is more than the God's law, though it cost him all of where he is living and his house. Provided that the thief is caught and the judges must be called to witness the deeds of the robber. Thieving is bad. The law of God is hard to try to stop people stealing. When a person steals, the whole process breaks down. The substance and communion breaks down before the Israelites, they were supposed to be 'milk and honey' and be rich in the Promised Land (see Numbers ch.13 v27).

Most plays and scripts we can watch require a robber to go to prison if he is caught. But there is not even one, who has to give up his whole house and property to make sure of what he has done. A robber takes away from Israel and breaks down the system where we currently lock the doors on our houses, our sheep and our barns.

- - - - - - - -

Certain women who had been healed of evil spirits and infirmities — Mary called Magdalene, out of whom had come seven demons, and Joanna the wife of Chuza, Herod's steward, and Susanna, and many others who provided for him from their substance. Luke ch.8 v2-3 (NKJV)

Certain women looked after Jesus as they thought it best to help him. He didn't have a home to rest in, he didn't have any money, because he was teaching the people and not working. Two Mary's, Joanna, Salome, Susanna and many others they were all ladies to let him go. Up and down the land of Israel and this is why they are mentioned. Quietly without fuss, they provided him with meals and only a few were listed in the Scriptures. They were there when he died (see Matthew ch.27 v55-56).

The women helped when he was dead and took him to the tomb. They bought spices so that they might anoint Jesus body and very early in the morning (Mark ch.16 v1-2). They were there to support Jesus in his ministry and they were there when the apostles were going to Jerusalem, after Jesus had been taken up before them to heaven (see Acts ch.1 v14). They were in the room when Peter spoke. The things that they did were to support him while he was on earth, they provided substance to help him.

- - - - - - - -

Now faith is the substance of things hoped for, the evidence of things not seen. Hebrews ch.11 v1 (NKJV)

In the New Testament, faith is what matters most. If you didn't have faith nobody could help you. Faith needs cars, ships and planes each one was constructed and you would climb in it expecting to go places. This is faith, we don't have to check anything, we rely on the engineers putting the things together. Even a building, road system or a bridge we expect them to be there. We have to have faith to believe in something.

This is true when we come to Jesus, we don't see him, but we trust in his work as recorded in the Bible. We trust in Jesus and put our substance at his disposal.

Tithes

Tithes taken as tenth part of the produce of the land and the stock taken from it.

The Lord said to Aaron, "You will have no inheritance in their land, nor will you have any share among them; I am you share and your inheritance among the Israelites. I give to the Levites all the other tithes in Israel as their inheritance in return for the work they do while serving at the Tent of Meeting," Numbers ch.18 v20-21

It is only valid in the Old Testament where God instituted a tithe for all the Israelite products. To give to the Levites because they didn't have any inheritance in the Promised Land (see 1 Chronicles ch.6 v1-3).

God said, 'I will remember you because you served me and the Levites because they had to do the work to set up God's temple'. Since the Levites as a whole and the priests in particular, had no part in the land that God was going to give it to them. It was necessary that the means for their provision must be well-documented.

God said to the Levites, "That is why I said concerning them: They will have no inheritance among the Israelite ... From these tithes you must give to the Lord's portion to Aaron the priest." Numbers ch.18 v24, v28

The Levites must also tithe and be given the part to the priests. The best and holiest part of everything that is presented to you. The produce of the threshing floor or the winepress (see Numbers ch.18 v30).

The people tithed and brought the goods to the Levite. Who subsequently tithed to give it to the priests. The Israelites tithed a tenth of their product to give it to the Levites. Who tithed and gave the best part to the priests? This was what God wanted them to do.

- - - - - - - -

Be sure to set aside a tenth of all that your fields produce each year ... so that you may learn to revere the Lord your God always. Deuteronomy ch.14 v22-23

It was a tenth of all that your fields produce. Each one had a duty to come up and give to the Levites the best part of all that comes from the land. So it was to revere the Lord your God who gave you the best share from the sun and rain. Each time you had your harvest, remember to give it to the Levites. The Levites gave the priests a share in what they had received from the people. It was a thank you for God's blessing for your land.

Then say to the Lord your God: "I have removed from my house the sacred portion and I have given it to the Levite, the alien, the fatherless and the widow, according to all you commanded. Deuteronomy ch.26 v13

Then recognise and celebrate the Levite, the alien, the fatherless and the widow to be as God instructed the people. The alien didn't have any home, or produce and certainly no land. He would come into the land of Palestine without anything at all. Remember that Israel was an alien, a slave coming into the Promised Land so give it back to another alien. The fatherless and the widow needed help because the man has died. The man who goes out to work in the fields is no longer there. The widow may have children to feed and she cares enough to let them survive. The fatherless and the widow need to be given plenty of crops to help them live.

This is what God commanded the people to do. The tithe must be given to the Levite, but it must be given to the alien, the fatherless and the widow as well.

- - - - - - - -

"Woe to you, teachers of the law and Pharisees, you hypocrites! You give a tenth of your spices - mint, dill and cummin. But you have neglected the more important matters of the law - justice, mercy and faithfulness. You should have practised the latter, without neglecting the former." Matthew ch.23 v23

In the New Testament it is the same as when Moses wrote the books of the law. The practice goes on, but it is widely different. We had teachers of the law and Pharisees, but there is every chance they were of different tribes and not Levites or priests. So the priests didn't have a share in what the Levite was tithing, nothing for the priests. It was a Jewish practice and not one for the believer who didn't have any fields nor any sheep nor crops. They all were instructed in the law of Israel but failed to do the right or proper thing.

They were not even aware of it they mocked Jesus and laughed at him even when he is carrying out his teaching from the word of God. Even when Jesus did miracles which they were not able to do, but they ridiculed and insulted him. Jesus said, 'Tithing is given over to justice, mercy and faithfulness.

They eventually stopped tithing the Promised Land, gave it to the holy temple where God was living in Jerusalem (see Luke ch.21 v1-4 and ch.19 v45-46).

- - - - - - - -

As he approached Jerusalem and saw the city, he wept over it and said, "If you, even you, had known on this day that would bring you peace - but now it is hidden from your eyes." Luke ch.19 v41-42

All Israel had ignored Jesus who would come and bring peace to all (see John ch.1 v11-12). He was saddened at the end of his life to see that even a big city Jerusalem did not give him any welcome. It wasn't tithing he was after, it was to let justice, mercy and faithfulness be there. That will give you peace from God. Peace that will be there for all time (see John ch.16 v33). But sadly it wasn't and Jesus was crucified out of the city.

ℐreasure

Treasure stored up anything of value to collect it for future use.

It is a noticeable difference from the Old Testament to the New Testament. For example:

Old Testament - God had Israel as his special possession.

New Testament - The treasure is giving to the poor.

Now if you obey me fully and keep my covenant, then out of all nations you will be my treasured possession. Although the whole earth is mine; you will be for me a kingdom of priests and a holy nation. Exodus ch.19 v5-6

God said to the Israelites while they were staying by Mount Sinai, provided you obey me fully, then I will give you out of my treasure. You can be my 'treasured possession'.

God said, 'The whole earth is mine' and I will look after you (see Deuteronomy ch.28 v1-14):

He will set you high above all the nations on earth.

He will be blessed in the city and the country.

He will bless the fruit of your womb.

He will look after the crops of your land.

He will care for your basket of produce.

He will grant that your enemies will be defeated against you.

He will give a blessing on everything you put your hand to.

He will send rain on your land in season.

He will give you power over the enemies.

He will look after you and you will be successful.

- - - - - - - -

To those who long for death that does not come, who search for it more than for hidden treasure. Job ch.3 v21

Satan afflicted Job with an enormous amount of trouble because Job respected God first, he would look after his children second. He is blameless and upright and was a treasure to God (see Job ch.1 v5, v8).

Job speaks out of the anguish he was in from Satan who cursed him. His friends could barely recognise him (see Job ch.2 v12). His wife said, 'Curse God and die'. So he sat among the ashes a symbol of mourning, sitting in the dust (see Job ch.2 v9-10). He took a piece of broken pottery and scrapped himself, he was covered in painful sores from the soles of his feet to the top of his head (see Job ch.2 v7-8). He considered giving up, but he was confident that God would rescue him. He remarked, 'Buried treasure is good but death is the only way'. It is a poor, sad man who Satan was determined to break him. He lost his children and all his homes were gone. Taken away, vanished by scoundrels and the mighty wind (see Job ch.1 v13-19).

What happened to Job, why did Satan do all that? Because God loved Job and he gave him back more things than he had previously been given (see Job ch.42 v10). God loved Job but he didn't prepare him for the trouble he was in and let Satan attack him and took his children away and covered him with boils. Job suffered awfully but God watched over him and then the storm arrived and God spoke to Job (see Job ch.37 v1-5).

Treasure is what God gives back to Job and he blessed him (see Job ch.42 v12-15).

- - - - - - - -

I collected great sums of silver and gold, the treasure of many kings and provinces. I hired wonderful singers, both men and women, and had many beautiful concubines. I had everything a man could desire! Ecclesiastes ch.2 v8 (NLT)

King Solomon collected all the things that he wanted: Silver and gold, wonderful singers, beautiful concubines. Treasure that surpassed even the best. However, he didn't find what he was looking for. Life not centred on God is purposeless and meaningless, without him nothing else can satisfy. He had cut himself off from God.

He didn't read the law of Mosaic every day or he wouldn't have done that with his wives or his horses (see Deuteronomy ch.17 v14-20). God said he would study it and read it every day, but king Solomon didn't. The start was king Solomon sacrificing all his animals and letting God know that he cared (see 1 Chronicles ch.5 v13), but in the end he let his foreign wives rule him and forgot God (see 1 Kings ch.11 v1-8).

Fear God and keep his commandments, for this is the duty of man. Ecclesiastes ch.12 v13

King Solomon said, 'Treasure in the Old Testament is obeying God'. Keeping God's laws and his duties and commandments. He made us and placed us on the earth, this is what we have to do, to live and prosper. But sadly, mankind had sinned and it all came tumbling down. Man, animals, trees and even the stars that shine at night.

- - - - - - - -

The caravan moves slowly across the terrible desert to Egypt—donkeys weighed down with riches and camels loaded with treasure—all to pay for Egypt's protection. Isaiah ch.30 v6 (NLT)

When Isaiah prophesied that there were two great kingdoms: Assyria and Egypt. Israel was caught between them, because the Mediterranean Sea from the west and the open desert to the east. There were two roads going through Palestine, either one the Kings Highway and the Via Maris. Palestine was in the middle from Egypt to Assyria.

The dry region in the southern parts of Palestine, perhaps it was necessary to use rickety paths because there was robbers and thieves in the wild regions. It is a picture of donkey weighing down with treasure to give to the Egypt to control Israel. This is not what God wanted, a picture of disobedience to obey him fully. This is what it would be like for the kings of Israel and Judah to having to go to the great kings for protection.

- - - - - - - -

For where your treasure is, there your heart will be also. Matthew ch.6 v21

The reason is that your heart will be close to your treasure. Not money or assets, but treasure. It involves all of that and more:

If it is money you will be conscious of only money.

If it is fortune you must think in your mind.

If its is possessions they will be everything you ever wanted.

If it is wealth you heart will overrule everybody and anything.

Your heart will only be conscious of your funds. Where does it go? Like the scheming 'Scrooge', he lost everything, marriage, office heating, bed clothes, house, poor people and he was tight-fisted with everybody.

Treasure leaves no room for God.

- - - - - - - -

Go, sell you possessions and give to the poor, and you will have treasure in heaven. Then come, follow me. Matthew ch.19 v21

Jesus said, 'Go and do it, sell all your rich possessions. There will always be poor and come and follow me' this is the chance we have, to decide. You will have treasure in heaven if you do it. God will decide and he will write it down in his book (see Revelation ch.20 v12). When we die then the books will be opened. We only have a small chance of this life on earth and it will be rewarded in heaven for ever and ever.

Treasure needs to be given to the poor. Why hang on to it? When we die it will be on the earth and we don't take it with us. Does it make you better? Does treasure at your disposal make you wise? Think about it, look at the rich persons are they really happy or joyful?

- - - - - - - -

We have this treasure in jars of clay to show that this all-surpassing power is from God and not from us. 2 Corinthians ch.4 v7

It was customary to store treasure in jars of clay, which had little value or beauty. Did not attract attention to themselves and their precious contents.

Here they represent human frailty and unworthiness. It is God who gives us treasure, and certainly not Satan who would try to get humans to be seen to be frail and unworthy and not even handle treasure.

This treasure you have accumulated will stand as evidence against you on the day of judgement. James ch.5 v3 (NLT)

This is from God and we respond by giving God back some treasure from us to avoid us when the day of judgement starts.

Not to be very poor, but to give what we don't need back to God. The treasure you have accumulated will be stacked against you when you have to face God in the day of judgement. What do we say to God?

- - - - - - - -

By doing this they will be storing up their treasure as a good foundation for the future so that they may experience true life. 1 Timothy ch.6 v19 (NLT)

Doing this will lead to a better life and we represent God in all things. Looking at your life, the clothes you wear, the food you eat and the drink you enjoy. We turn to God and ask him to supply what we need (see Matthew ch.6 v25-34).

This treasure we don't really need, we can pass it on to the next generation. It is not life as such, but we need it to be ready to let it go. This is 'true life' from God when we trust God for everything. Food, drink and clothes which will always come to us.

Be perfect, therefore, as your heavenly Father is perfect. Matthew ch.5 v48

Jesus sets up the high ordeal of perfect love, not that we can obtain it for ourselves. This is God's high standard for us, helped by the Holy Spirit who will come into the believer's mind and heart. We can only do that by giving treasure away to the poor, giving what you need for yourself. Its the word 'treasure' to be stored away in the bank or shares that might reward you.

Valuables

Valuables refers to value as worth which renders anything useful or excellent.

'But about this time tomorrow I will send my officials to search your palace and the homes of your people. They will take away everything you consider valuable!'
1 Kings ch.20 v6 (NLT)

Ben-Hadad, king of Aram mustered his whole army with thirty-two kings and he went up to attack Samaria. He sent messengers to Ahab king of Israel, saying, 'Your silver and gold, the best of your wives and children are mine' (see 1 Kings ch.20 v1-3).

The elders and the people of the land all answered, 'Don't listen to him or agree to his demands'. The prophet said, 'Do you see this vast army? God will give it into your hand today'. King Ahab had only 232 officers and it is not a large military force but it was a city under siege (see 1 Kings ch.20 v13-15). Because they were totally surrounded and if you looked over the wall and the army was still waiting there, looking aggressive, even 32 kings!

The word of the Lord rather than from king Ahab's own military strength. Valuables were taken by Aram's own people to emphasise his superior strength over Israel.

- - - - - - - -

King Jehoshaphat and his men went out to gather the plunder. They found vast amounts of equipment, clothing, and other valuables—more than they could carry. There was so much plunder that it took them three days just to collect it all! 2 Chronicles ch.20 v25 (NLT)

Later, when the men of Judah came to the place that overlooks the desert and looked towards the vast army. They only saw dead bodies lying on the ground; no-one had escaped (see 2 Chronicles ch.20 v24). King Jehoshaphat had defeated Moab and Ammon. He stood out for a wise, just ruler and he strengthened his kingdom. Not in Israel as such, but close to the Dead Sea where there was grass for the sheep. In Judah down south.

There was so much valuables that it will take three days to collect it. There was a lot of treasure!

- - - - - - - -

Hezekiah had very great riches and honour, and he made treasuries for his silver and gold and for his precious stones, spices, shields and all kinds of valuables. 2 Chronicles ch.32 v27

King Hezekiah had a lot of valuables, everything he could want and more. He was a good king and reigned for twenty-nine years (see 2 Chronicles ch.29 v1-2). However, he became ill and was at the point of death. He prayed to God and wept bitterly because he wanted to live (see 2 Kings ch.20 v1-3). The Lord said, 'He would let him have another fifteen years' (2 Kings ch.20 v6).

During those fifteen years Hezekiah had a son named Manasseh (see 2 Kings ch.21 v1). Manasseh did more evil in his time than all the other kings before him, it was a dreadful time for the people, so they forgot about God (2 Kings ch.21 v2-16). The Lord knew when he added 15 years to king Hezekiah's life that his son would cause the whole people to turn from him.

Valuables do not protect the rulers from being kind and honouring God.

- - - - - - - -

On the fourth day after our arrival, the silver, gold, and other valuables were weighed at the Temple of our God and entrusted to Meremoth son of Uriah the priest and to Eleazar son of Phinehas, along with Jozabad son of Jeshua and Noadiah son of Binnui—both of whom were Levites. Ezra ch.8 v33 (NLT)

When the remnant of Judah returned to the Promised Land after being exiled or captured by King Nebuchadnezzar. The Medes took possession of Babylon and then they didn't want people being exiled miles away from their homes. They had a long journey home for about nine hundred miles, going through the desert regions back to the Promised Land. The priest Ezra arrived back in Jerusalem followed by Nehemiah who was cup-bearer to the king Artaxerxes.

The valuables needed protection from God as we arrived. He guarded us from enemies and bandits along the way (see Ezra ch.8 v31). Everything was accounted for by number and was recorded at that same time (see Ezra ch.8 v34). The valuables were entrusted to the Levites who were there to do service for the Lord, the God of Israel.

.

- - - - - - - -

So don't be afraid; you are more valuable to God than a whole flock of sparrows. Matthew ch.10 v31 (NLT)

Why are sparrows mentioned? Only because they were poor and needed a nest in the houses where the people lived and they were offered by sale in Palestine. The sparrow is not intensely coloured nor brightly textured, there is always a look out for when the sparrow feeds or comes to drink. They have a group arrangement. One looks after the other, like starlings.

Man is like that and nobody could call him beautiful. He is only got hair over much of his body, no brightly coloured skin and nothing textured. He falls over a lot and he is not able to lift heavy things, this is why we have hospitals. But God thinks of him as beautiful a valuable treasure. He was made like God himself (see Genesis ch.1 v26).

- - - - - - - -

I once thought these things were valuable, but now I consider them worthless because of what Christ has done. Yes, everything else is worthless when compared with the infinite value of knowing Christ Jesus my Lord. Philippians ch.3 v7-8 (NLT)

Almost all valuables are worthless compared with what Jesus has done. His sacrificial work on the cross to bear our sins before God. We were helpless but he will come and save us. Valuables are worthless because of what Jesus has done. We are his instruments going out preaching and teaching the message that Jesus, God's only Son has taught us.

He saved us, not because of righteous things we had done, but because of his mercy. Titus ch.3 v5

Valuables cannot be used to save us. They are there on the earth and when we die, we leave them behind. Gold, silver, precious stones, spices and the rest. We are only there for a brief season and after that we must face the judgement. God has written down all that we have done. Valuables will not be there at all, we can't find a way to let ourselves off from God, we are only there to be judged, whether good or bad.

If we don't face the judgement on earth, then we will be sure to pay for the work when God faces us. He will only do what his books have contained, that is all. The 'righteous things' we have done with his Holy Spirit who guides us and leads us. It is his mercy that we will be saved, it is like a voice in our mind to remind us of what he wants us to do.

Wealth

Wealth is a valuable possession of any kind.

He became a very rich man, and his wealth continued to grow. He acquired so many flocks of sheep and goats, herds of cattle, and servants that the Philistines became jealous of him. Genesis ch.26 v13-15 (NLT)

Issac planted crops in that land and they produced an outstanding harvest and his sheep and goats they prospered because the Lord blessed him. Even the Philistines became envious of him. Isaac was obedient to God's will and he was mindful of the covenant promises from God to Abraham.

The Philistines had all the fresh soil along the Mediterranean Sea and they should have plenty of growth. In Palestine, there are great differences in altitude within short distances. These contrast between the dry Arebah at the edge of the desert with its rugged places and opposite are the fertile and watered areas of the Trans-Jordan. Wealth comes from God and he gave it to the Israelites.

- - - - - - - -

Esau had his livestock and cattle—all the wealth he had acquired in the land of Canaan—and moved away from his brother, Jacob. There was not enough land to support them both because of all the livestock and possessions they had acquired. Genesis ch.36 v6-7 (NLT)

There were two people: Esau and Jacob whose livestock were such that they had to move apart. There was not the land to support them both. Amazing only two brothers! We have in Israel, the Promised Land where thousands who gather together. There is only enough water and the sheep filled the land. They drilled wells and it is still true in the New Testament (see John ch.4 v6). The brothers had plenty of sheep more than we could count today, that is why they moved apart.

This was good arable land with plenty of sun, it was known as the 'Fertile Crescent' from Egypt to the Ararat past the Euphrates and Tigris Rivers. Between the Mediterranean Sea and the Wilderness of Edom and Moab.

- - - - - - - -

He did all this so you would never say to yourself, 'I have achieved this wealth with my own strength and energy.' Remember the Lord your God. He is the one who gives you power to be successful, in order to fulfil the covenant, he confirmed to your ancestors with an oath. Deuteronomy ch.8 v17-18 (NLT)

Moses did say that only wealth comes from God. If one has achieved this wealth by his own strength and energy, that is not strictly true. You forgot to remember the Lord your God. Only if you obey the Lord and keep his commandments then he will bless you. Otherwise, you work but hard but things don't work out for you. Remember his instructions for the Israelites: (see Deuteronomy ch.28 v15-68)

You will be cursed in the city and country.

Your basket will only be empty.

You will not be able to bear children.

You will see the crops of the land wither.

You will watch as your calves and lambs die.

You will be cursed when you come in and go out.

You will be plagued with diseases.

You will have fever and inflammation.

You will notice no rain comes on your land.

You will be defeated with your enemies.

You will hand over your sons and daughters to another.

You will be forced to exile the land.

You will notice that the alien is above you.

You will be forced to defend your cities.

You will be slaves and destroyed.

That is what happened to Israel and Judea they were taken away to suffer like the exiled people. For many kings from king Saul to king Hosea in Israel, eighteen kings were evil and three kings were good. From king Rehoboam to king Zedekiah in Judea, ten kings were evil and ten kings were good. The prophets said it would happen but the people didn't care they forgot about God. They were happy and content to let the world drift by. They were exiled to Assyria and Babylon. Only in Judea, a few returned back to the Promised Land.

- - - - - - - -

Haman boasted to them about his vast wealth, his many sons, and all the ways the king had honoured him and how he had elevated him about the other nobles and officials. Esther ch.5 v11

When the exile happened to Israel and Judah, they were transported away but they lived in Persia stretching from India to Cush (see Esther ch.1 v1).

Later, King Xerxes promoted Haman and elevated him higher than all the other nobles; they knelt down and paid homage to him. Haman asked the king, 'If it pleases the king let a decree be issued to wipe out those customs are different from ours, I will give you ten thousand talents of silver into the king's hands' (see Esther ch.3 v8-9). He realised that Mordecai didn't bow down to him and he was determined to rid of all his people, like the Jews.

Wealth is only used for good, not for evil. Haman was hanged (see Esther ch.7 v9-10) because he forgot Queen Esther who was one of those affected by his authority and his scheming plan. However great you are, something you have forgotten may make you a target of the enemies.

- - - - - - - -

The seed that fell among the thorns represents those who hear God's word, but all too quickly the message is crowded out by the worries of this life and the lure of wealth, so no fruit is produced. Matthew ch.13 v22 (NLT)

We have noted this before. But God's seed is like the message about the kingdom that was sowed by the farmer. Some fell on the path, rocky places, thorns and the good soil.

So what happened to the thorns? The message is unfruitful by the worries of this life and the lure of wealth. We all go to the shops, pass by and don't look at the preacher who explains the word of God. We need goods and will look in the windows for them. If the price is too expensive, we go on looking. We forget and overlook the preacher. We need a new part, something is broken and your mind is fixed only for that part, everything else is forgotten and overlooked.

It all goes together worries and wealth and no fruit is produced. There is not much time. Sadly, we ignore the preacher who could lead us for what we do when we die? Do you know what will happen when you go to Hades?

- - - - - - - -

Meanwhile, Zacchaeus stood before the Lord and said, "I will give half my wealth to the poor, Lord, and if I have cheated people on their taxes, I will give them back four times as much!" Luke ch.19 v8 (NLT)

Zacchaeus was a chief tax collector and was wealthy (see Luke ch.19 v2). He made money out of the people and only gave a small amount to the Romans. That is why he was so rich. The people really hated him because he would take what they had for taxes (see Luke ch.19 v7).

He was in a tree because he was short and nobody thought about his need. Jesus went up to him and said Zacchaeus, 'I must stay at your house today'. Zacchaeus said to all the people:

'I will give half my wealth to the poor.

If I have cheated any one on their taxes.

I will give them back for times as much'.

This was true salvation. He gave back more than he should have in the Mosaic Law (see Exodus ch.22 v9). His action gave a lot more than he should have to those who was affected by his decisions. Most of his wealth was gone to the poor.

- - - - - - - -

Yet true godliness with contentment is itself great wealth. After all, we brought nothing with us when we came into the world, and we can't take anything with us when we leave it. So if we have enough food and clothing, let us be content. 1 Timothy ch.6 v6-8 (NLT)

When we die all of the wealth we possess doesn't go with us. The Egyptians thought it did. But when we dig in the pyramids, we find all of the wealth is there, or the robbers have taken it away over the past few years. We arrive empty handed and we go back to the Lord as souls totally naked.

If we have food and clothing let us be content with that. Wealth is only what we have on this earth. We arrive with nothing and we depart from his world as souls back to God. Nothing goes with us, not even a picture, nor a wedding ring.

- - - - - - - - -

You have hoarded wealth in the last days. Look! The wages you failed to pay the workmen who mowed your fields are crying out against you. The cries of the harvesters have reached the ears of the Lord Almighty. You have lived on earth in luxury and self-indulgence. You have fattened yourself in the day of slaughter. You have condemned and murdered innocent men, who were not opposing you. James ch.5 v3-6

True wealth means we get more and more and leave the other people to manage as best they can. No one can say that wealth is bad, but use it properly as Zacchaeus did.

Warning to rich oppressors:

You have hoarded wealth in the last days.

You have failed to pay for the workmen and harvesters.

You have lived on this life in luxury.

You have been living in self-indulgence.

You have fattened yourself like animals.

You have condemned and murdered innocent men.

Wealth in the last days. Is that you, who are treating the poor like that? Shame on you, so what are you saying to God when you are judged before the great white throne? (see Revelation ch.20 v11)

Well-being

Well-being as welfare, satisfaction and comfortable living.

Nothing is left for him to eat; therefore, his well-being will not last. In his self-sufficiency he will be in distress; every hand of misery will come against him. Job ch.20 v21-22 (NKJV)

His well-being will not last for ever. In his greed nothing will be left for him to eat. He will be in distress and every hand of misery will be on him. So what happened? Each of his three friends, they pointed out that Job was in trouble from God. Then they pestered him again, each man had a point which Job had apparently overlooked.

This is the work of Zophar the Naamathite, he suggested that a man was weak because God had punished him. But he forgot that Satan had scourged him. God was angry with his three friends because they have not spoken of the Lord what is right and proper (see Job ch.42 v7).

- - - - - - - -

When Sanballat the Horonite and Tobiah the Ammonite official heard of it, they were deeply disturbed that a man had come to seek the well-being of the children of Israel. Nehemiah ch.2 v10 (NKJV)

After the exile, the people returned to the Promised Land. They were going to Jerusalem to rebuild the temple of the Lord, build up the broken-down walls and mend the gates. Sanballat was the governor over Samaria and Tobiah had a close relationship with Eliashib the priest (see Nehemiah ch.13 v4-5). He was probably the governor of Trans-Jordan under the Persians.

The reasons why Sanballat and Tobiah were not really religious but political. The authority of the governor was threatened by Nehemiah's arrival. The two governors who were running the country. They didn't have the right to halt and abandon Nehemiah, they were simply aliens or Jews coming into Palestine. So the two of them stopped the work. The work of rebuilding Jerusalem came from the attack by them, they wrote letters to the king of Persia and did all they could to hamper the work. The well-being of Nehemiah was not taken into consideration.

- - - - - - - -

Let no one seek his own, but each one the other's well-being.   1 Corinthians ch.10 v24 (NKJV)

It is a matter of concern not to stop the well-being of others whether they are important, or have gifts that we don't have. Or are successful in their own right. We have a duty not to compare himself with someone else for each man should carry his own load (see Galatians ch.6 v4-5). This means we all have a job to do and different abilities to carry out the work. The women who worked hard to let the Lord do his job they were there at his execution (see Matthew ch.27 v55). Only two women were watching where he was buried in his tomb (see Matthew ch.27 v61). All the believers were locked in their houses (see John ch.20 v18-19).

All the work is special and unique. All the different skills we have and do the Lord's work, where we are based and located. Nobody could do your talent and expertise. If you don't do it, nobody else can. Think about it. The Lord has chosen you as a believer, and given you the Holy Spirit to aid and instruct you. You have a work to do for the kingdom of God. Only you can achieve this, wherever you go, whatever you achieve. God has selected you and he is looking for you to aid and complete his work. This is why you are still alive!

Don't worry if the work of the missionary away in a country not his own, or the evangelist who works to get people to Jesus or the minister who runs a church. But think of the women?

They were there to encourage Jesus.

They decided he was provided for meals.

They were there while he was executed.

They sought him outside his tomb.

They were indeed running to his disciples.

Jesus came up to them and spoke to them. He was the first to explain that he had been risen from the dead. Each one had a ministry that only you can do.

Go and do likewise, for God has selected you.

www.ingramcontent.com/pod-product-compliance
Lightning Source LLC
Chambersburg PA
CBHW051533120626
46551CB00012B/1207